FACTS
& RECORDS
AMAZING
ACHIEVEMENTS

FACTS & RECORDS

AMAZING ACHIEVEMENTS

KINGFISHER

NEW YORK

Art Editor   Keith Davis
Editor   Matthew Turner
Coordinating Editor   Caitlin Doyle

Art Director   Mike Davis
DTP Coordinator   Sarah Pfitzner

Production Controllers   Jo Blackmore, Kelly Johnson

Artwork Archivists   Wendy Allison, Steve Robinson

KINGFISHER
a Houghton Mifflin Company imprint
215 Park Avenue South
New York, New York 10003
www.houghtonmifflinbooks.com

Produced by Davis/Turner Packaging

First published in 2003

10 9 8 7 6 5 4 3 2 1

1TR(SBF)/0103/TWP/MA(MA)/SMA150

LIBRARY OF CONGRESS CATALOGING-IN-PUBLICATION DATA
has been applied for.

ISBN 0-7534-5453-X

Printed in Singapore

CONTENTS

CIVILIZATION

COMMUNICATION 6, FOOD AND SHELTER 8,
COMMERCE 10, LAWS AND JUSTICE 12, LEADERS 14,
HEROES 16, PHILOSOPHIES AND RELIGIONS 18

CULTURE

LITERATURE 20, PERFORMING ARTS 22,
VISUAL ARTS 24, MOVIES 26, MUSIC 28

SCIENCE & TECHNOLOGY

UNIVERSAL LAWS 30, VITAL DISCOVERIES 32,
CRUCIAL INVENTIONS 34, MEDICAL BREAKTHROUGHS 36

ENGINEERING

ROAD AND RAIL 38, SEA AND AIR 40,
BUILDINGS AND MONUMENTS 42, MIGHTY STRUCTURES 44

SPORTS

THE OLYMPICS 46, ON THE TEAM 48,
SPORTS LEGENDS 50

EXPLORATION & ENDURANCE

EARLY PIONEERS 52, GREAT ADVENTURERS 54, INTO SPACE 56,
BEYOND THE LIMITS 58

GLOSSARY 60, INDEX 62, ACKNOWLEDGMENTS 64

COMMUNICATION

Communication is the sharing of information. It allows people to pass on ideas and work together. Few human achievements would have been possible without effective forms of communication.

Language

People communicate mostly by speaking and writing. No one knows when human speech first developed, but prehistoric people probably spoke to each other by imitating sounds in nature. Cave drawings were the first steps toward a written language, but as people began living in towns they needed a more accurate way to identify possessions and keep records. Around 3,500 B.C. the Sumerians, who lived in the Middle East, developed a writing system where pictures stood for objects and common ideas. Later the ancient Greeks used similar symbols as the basis for their alphabet.

DOWN ON PAPER
People use writing to spread thoughts and ideas. Early books, such as this bible, were used to communicate religious ideas to large numbers of people.

ALPHABET
Around 800 B.C. the Greeks created the first alphabet. Instead of representing an object, each Greek symbol stood for a sound in the language. As a result, the Greeks could write any word that they spoke.

In Chinese writing some symbols represent sounds, while others depict objects or ideas.

FACTS AND FIGURES

There are 6,000 languages spoken in the world today. 200 of them have over one million speakers each.

The first transatlantic telephone cable was laid in 1956 between Scotland and Newfoundland in Canada.

Scotsman John Logie Baird gave the first practical demonstration of television technology in 1925.

The Internet began in 1984. By 2001 there were 250 million people connecting to it regularly worldwide.

Sending messages

Until electronic communications became common people used systems of signals to send messages. Early peoples used runners or men on horseback to carry spoken messages. Drums and fires were used to signal basic messages such as "enemy in sight." In the 1700s and 1800s people used semaphore and heliography to send more complex messages. Semaphore, developed by Frenchman Claude Chappe in 1791, is a visual signaling code in which two flags or pointers can be positioned to stand for different letters or numbers. A heliographer uses a set of mirrors that reflect sunlight to an observer in a series of coded flashes.

PIGEON MAIL
People used to train pigeons to take messages from one place to another. A message was tied to the bird's leg.

PUT A KNOT IN IT
The Incas, a native South American people, used smoke to send signals. Instead of writing, they knotted strings called *quipu* to keep records.

Early telecommunications

In the early 1800s scientists found that electrical impulses could be used to transmit signals along a wire. In 1835 American Samuel Morse used the process in the first efficient telegraph system. In 1876 Scottish-born Alexander Graham Bell invented the telephone by turning sound waves into electrical currents and transmitting them. Ten years later Germany's Heinrich Hertz showed that sound waves could be converted into electromagnetic waves. A receiving antenna some distance away received these and converted them back into sound. It was the birth of radio and mass communication.

MAN ON THE RADIO
Italian Guglielmo Marconi built the first practical radio in 1901. Within 20 years a single radio transmitter could broadcast to thousands of people.

The Internet began as an experiment to see if a computer network could survive a nuclear attack.

MORSE CODE TRANSMITTER
Samuel Morse invented Morse Code, a telegraph code that uses short "dots" and longer "dashes" to represent letters.

Modern communications

For most of us television is the most familiar form of mass communication. Television pictures are carried in a similar way to radio, which means they need many transmitting stations to reach a wide area. It takes time to send pictures and sound over great distances. Satellites have solved the problem. They can relay several TV programs or thousands of telephone calls at the same time.

The greatest achievement in communications is the development of the Internet, a vast computer network with information on almost every topic. It can be accessed by anyone with a computer and a modem, which enables the computer to send and receive information on a household telephone line.

ON THE MOVE
The Internet links governments, companies, and individuals all over the world. Mobile Internet technology means that we can even access the Internet from handheld devices such as cellular phones.

DATABANK

Q When was the first public television broadcast, and where did it take place?

A The first broadcast took place in 1936 at the BBC's station in London, England.

Q Why did the Greek alphabet replace the pictorial writing systems of earlier peoples?

A Most pictorial writing systems are very inflexible and cannot easily adapt new words.

BEAM ME UP
A satellite dish on the ground beams up radio signals to a satellite that orbits above the same part of Earth at all times.

RECEIVING
The satellite relays the radio signals to a computer in another part of the world almost instantaneously.

FOOD AND SHELTER

Food and shelter are our primary needs. When early peoples found ways of building houses and harvesting crops, they laid the foundations and sowed the seeds for the world's great civilizations.

Early farmers

No one is sure exactly when agriculture began, but by about 9,000 B.C. farmers were growing barley, oats, millet, and wheat. They used simple tools such as the digging stick, hoe, and scythe (a blade that cuts grass). Around 8,000 B.C. farmers living in Mesopotamia (modern-day Iraq) and Egypt invented the plow. This revolutionized agriculture—a farmer with a horse-drawn plow could turn over long lines of soil with ease, doing the work of several workers with hand tools.

On large farms today farmers use light aircraft to dust their crops with chemicals that boost growth and kill pests.

EARTH MOVERS
Early farmers hauled their own plows. Later they harnessed oxen and horses. Animal-drawn plows are still used in parts of some continents such as Africa.

MAKING WORK EASIER
In 1838 American Hyram Moor invented the self-propelled combine. It cut and beat corn much faster than horse-drawn reapers did.

BREAD BASKET
In 1982 American company Monsanto made the first GM (genetically modifed) plant. GM crops grow quickly and are better at resisting pests and disease. They may keep the world fed, but not everyone agrees they are good for our health or the environment.

NATURE'S BOUNTY
Medieval farmers kept birds for eggs, pigs for meat, and cows and goats for milk and hides. Straw served as animal bedding and as a dry roofing material.

DATABANK

Q When and where are humans thought to have first appeared?

A The first humans lived on East Africa's plains 4–6 million years ago.

Q Which cities have the largest populations?

A Tokyo (Japan), New York (U.S.), and Seoul (South Korea).

Q Where were windmills first used to grind grain into flour?

A Windmills came from 7th-century western Asia—probably Syria.

Q Why is organic food seen as healthy and environmentally friendly?

A It's produced without harmful chemicals or cruelty to animals.

BIOSPHERE 2
Inside this huge greenhouse in the Sonoran Desert in Arizona scientists have created replicas of seven major world habitats, including a rain forest, a savanna, and even a 1.2 million-gallon saltwater ocean.

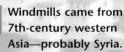

We know how medieval monks farmed because they kept detailed records of daily life in the form of diaries and paintings.

Animals on farms

Our earliest ancestors were hunter-gatherers. Always on the move, they picked fruits and nuts and hunted wild animals with spears and arrows. Tens of thousands of years later people began keeping goats and pigs for a steady supply of meat. They used oxen and horses to plow fields and carry loads. In 19th-century Europe many people moved to cities to work in industry, but they still needed farms for their food. Milk and meat were sent to markets by train, a new invention. Today, in order to meet the soaring demand for food, some farms are run like factories.

DRINK UP
We drink milk from cows, goats, and buffalo. Each year an average cow gives 1,560 gallons of milk. This is a Holstein-Friesland, a European breed that produces 90 percent of all milk drunk in the United States.

WILD WEST
Cowboys are very good at rounding up cattle—a team of just eight can control a herd of 2,500.

FACTORY FARM
Some mother pigs never leave their pen. Factory farming is efficient, but many people think it is cruel.

FACTS AND FIGURES

Çatal Hüyük, in south-central Turkey, is the site of a Stone Age settlement dating back almost 9,000 years.

One million years ago early humans discovered fire. They used it to keep warm, cook meat, and scare away animals.

In 1939 scientists developed the chemical DDT to kill crop pests. It is now widely banned because it is so poisonous.

A roof over your head

The first artificial dwellings were huts built from mud, sticks, and grass. In the 300s B.C. the Sumerians built the world's first cities on the fertile floodplains of Mesopotamia. Along the Indus Valley (now part of Pakistan and India) another people flourished from 2,500 B.C. to 1,700 B.C. The ancient world's biggest cities were Alexandria in Egypt and the ancient Greek city Ephesus. Both were centers of scholarship and science. Around 50 B.C. the Romans devised drains and central heating. Today there are megacities. For example, Tokyo, Japan's capital, houses around 34 million people— more than triple the world population of 10,000 years ago!

HARAPPA
Along with Mohenjo-Daro this was one of the two major cities of the Indus Valley people. Its living quarters and granaries surrounded a fortified citadel.

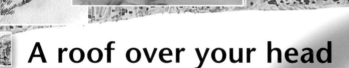

Venice, Italy's island city, is a maze of winding canals and streets. It was the wealthiest seaport in medieval Europe.

MACHU PICCHU
This high-altitude town in Peru, built by the Inca civilization, escaped discovery by 16th-century Spanish invaders.

COMMERCE

Money may not be everything, but it has been the driving force behind every mighty civilization and giant company.

SAFEKEEPING
This medieval private banker would have exchanged foreign currencies as well as providing clients with a cash deposit and withdrawal service.

Exchanging goods

Throughout history people have used all types of odd objects for barter and exchange, including shells, beads, precious metals, and cattle. But as trade between rulers and merchants increased they needed a standard way of doing deals so that it was easy to compare the values of different goods. Around 700 B.C. coins were invented by King Gyges of Lydia, a small kingdom that is now part of Turkey. Before long other nations had introduced their own form of currency.

OLD MONEY
Roman coins were made of bronze alloy (a blend of metals) or silver and had pictures of gods, rulers, or special insignia.

The first credit cards in the 1920s were like today's store cards—each was used with a single company such as a hotel chain.

International trade flourished in the Middle Ages. In the 1700s the first modern banks appeared where merchants could deposit and borrow money. The London Stock Exchange opened in 1801, enabling people to invest money in companies and trade their investments with one another. Many capital cities now have a stock exchange, which plays a major part in the world economy.

NEW YORK STOCK EXCHANGE
At the stock exchange traders buy shares in companies, hoping their value will rise. It's a risky business because values can also fall.

DATABANK

Q	What is a patent?	**A**	It is a legal document that controls the right to make and sell a product.
Q	What is free trade?	**A**	It describes international trade with minimal government control.
Q	What did the United States do in its Marshall Plan of 1947–1951?	**A**	It gave $13 billion in aid to the war-damaged countries of Europe.
Q	What is income tax?	**A**	Money we give to the government to go toward running the country.

E-COMMERCE
With a credit card and access to the Internet you can buy all kinds of products and services through a computer. But E-commerce still has a long way to go. In 2001 just three percent of the world's population had access to the Internet, and New York alone had more Internet accounts than all of Africa.

Trading places

The first great traders were the Phoenicians, seafarers based in the eastern Mediterranean (modern-day Lebanon and Syria) in the first millennium B.C. In the 1400s and 1500s Europeans discovered North America, India, and Southeast Asia. From these lands coffee, tobacco, sugar, and spices flooded into Europe. Spain and Portugal created overseas empires to profit from the growth of commerce; the British, French, and Dutch did also. In the 1800s industrialized nations exported manufactured goods such as clothes, shoes, and tools to their colonies. In return they imported food and raw materials such as cotton, timber, and minerals.

Rotterdam-Europoort, in the Netherlands, is the world's largest shipping port. It links the Meuse and Rhine rivers to the North Sea.

PHOENICIAN TRADING VOYAGE
The Phoenicians exported timber, cloth, glass, and metalwork. They traded for such goods as metals, jewels, papyrus, and ivory.

Big business

Giant companies, such as Microsoft and Mitsubishi, are global—they have factories and offices around the world. They use modern communications and fast transportation to sell products and services. A giant company takes advantage of local economic conditions in different countries. This way it can produce goods where wages are lowest and then export them to richer markets. Big companies grow even bigger as they buy out rival companies in order to increase their market share.

Many people claim that giant companies abuse the environment and exploit the poor in order to make a profit. In response the companies argue that operating globally is the only way they can sell goods to us at the low prices we demand.

VERY BIG MAC
American milkshake salesman Ray Kroc opened the first McDonald's restaurant in 1955 in Des Plaines, Illinois. Today there are more than 29,000 McDonald's in 121 countries around the world.

HEALTH WEALTH
GlaxoSmithKline is one of the world's biggest companies; most of its profit comes from the sale of medicine.

FACTS AND FIGURES

In the souks (markets) of North Africa and the Middle East traders often decide the price of goods by bargaining.

World trade is controlled by governments and by global bodies such as the World Trade Organization (WTO).

A new currency called the euro officially replaced 12 national currencies in Europe in 2002.

GAME ON!
Rivalry between companies, such as the makers of video game consoles, forces them to be creative and also to reduce prices.

BURIED TREASURE
Oil fuels many of the world's industries and is vital to the economy. Saudi Arabia has the largest oil reserves of any country.

LAWS AND JUSTICE

Every civilized society needs a legal system for keeping the peace. Laws protect the rights of civilians, help settle disputes, and deter people from crime.

HAMMURABI
This Babylonian king ruled from 1792–1750 B.C. He collected a set of Sumerian laws known as a code. His code, based on 282 case decisions, was carved on a pillar that is now exhibited in France's Louvre Museum.

Legal systems

Once, chiefs and kings were in charge of justice in their lands. Solomon, king of Israel from 970–930 B.C. was famous for his wisdom in settling disputes. Later rulers passed down their legal duties to officials, who in effect were the ancestors of today's judges. The Greeks and Romans were the first civilizations to use lawyers—experts in law who, for a fee, argued in court on behalf of citizens.

Today, Great Britain uses a system called common law, first adopted in the Middle Ages and now also used in the U.S. Continental Europe, South America, and parts of Africa and Asia use a system known as civil law.

Legal systems are continually updated in order to make them fair and just for everyone.

WHEN IN ROME . . .
Most Western legal systems are based on Roman law, first begun 2,450 years ago. Here, Lucius Sulla (Rome's dictator 82–79 B.C.) is decreeing new laws.

The death penalty is no longer used in Europe. China, many African nations, and 38 of the 52 U.S. states still use it.

GOD'S COMMAND
The Koran (above) is the basis for *shariah*, or Islamic law. Christians try to live by God's Ten Commandments.

INDEPENDENT THINKING
The signing of the Declaration of Independence on July 4, 1776 ended British rule in the U.S. A later paper, the Constitution (1787), laid down U.S. law.

FACTS AND FIGURES

The principles of Roman law, the first modern legal system, were used until the fall of the Byzantine Empire in 1453.

The Magna Carta, issued by King John in 1215, was one of the first charters to define the liberties of English citizens.

On August 28, 1963 more than 200,000 people marched on Washington, D.C. to protest against racism.

Setting the world to rights

It may seem strange, but there are laws to govern warfare between nations. For example, the first Geneva Convention was signed in 1864 to protect the wounded on the battlefield. Today it also controls the use of chemical weapons and the treatment of prisoners. Those who break the rules of war face punishment. At a mass trial in Nuremberg, Germany (1945–1946), 22 Nazis were charged with war crimes.

At The Hague, in the Netherlands, there is now a permanent International Tribunal. It was here in 2001 that Slobodan Milosevic, the former president of Yugoslavia, became the first head of state to be charged with crimes against humanity.

The United Nations, founded in 1945, promotes international peace and security and protects basic human rights.

NUREMBERG TRIALS
Hermann Göring, Rudolf Hess, and Joachim von Ribbentrop were tried for war crimes. Göring killed himself, Hess went to jail, and von Ribbentrop was hanged.

People power

Revolutions are dramatic examples of "people power" at work. In France in 1789 the peasant class overthrew the ruling class. In 1804, after the revolution, Napoleon Bonaparte proclaimed a new French empire with a new set of laws. His Napoleonic Code swept away unfair laws and brought equal rights for all.

In Russia in 1917 the people toppled the czar (emperor) and his corrupt government, and the Bolshevik party took over.

History is also full of revolts against unjust laws. Until the 1900s women in most countries did not have the right to vote. In England, Emmeline Pankhurst (1858–1928) and her daughter Christabel campaigned for this right. In 1918 British women aged 30 and over were finally allowed to vote, and in 1928 the age was lowered to 21. In the 1960s civil rights campaigners protested against the racism that marred American society. Their inspiring African-American leader, Martin Luther King, Jr., paid with his life when he was shot dead in 1968.

OFF WITH THEIR HEADS!
In 1789 angry French peasants rebelled against the nobles and executed many of them. They even killed King Louis XVI.

FIERY WOMAN
Emmeline Pankhurst was often imprisoned in her fight for women's rights in the 1880s–1920s. In the 1960s U.S. feminists, such as Betty Friedan and Gloria Steinem, continued the campaign for women's equality.

The Universal Declaration of Human Rights (1948) includes the right to a fair trial and freedom of thought, expression, and religion.

ACTION FOR ANIMALS
Special laws protect threatened animals like whales and tigers. One of the most important is CITES, signed in 1973 to control international trade in wildlife.

FIGHTING SLAVERY
In the past the use of African slaves on plantations made many landowners rich. But increasingly, slavery was seen as a cruel abuse of human rights. It was banned in the British Empire in 1833 and in 1865 in the U.S. Sadly, slavery and child labor remain common in many countries.

LEADERS

Great leadership requires special qualities. We remember the best leaders for their wise use of power, fair treatment of people, and skillful negotiating in world affairs.

PEACEMAKER
After spending 27 years in prison Nelson Mandela became South Africa's first black president in 1994. He brought hope to the country's black majority population and unity to a land long divided by racial hatred.

Great statespeople

Leaders who work for the good of their nation are said to be great statespeople. Julius Caesar, for example, strengthened the Roman Empire in the 1st century A.D. An excellent military leader, he was also a crafty politician and a careful administrator. In the 1780s George Washington rebuilt America after the chaos left by civil war. He helped draft a new constitution (the laws of the nation), and in 1789 he became the first U.S. president. From 1740–1786 King Frederick II built up Prussia (a former German kingdom) into a major European power.

ABLE MAN
U.S. president during the 1861–1865 Civil War, Abraham Lincoln saved the Union and fought against slavery.

GREAT SOUL
Peace-loving Mohandas K. Gandhi steered India toward independence from British rule. India achieved that goal in 1948, the year of Gandhi's death.

Chou En-lai, premier of China from 1949–1976, was a stable influence on his country in a troubled era.

GOOD QUEEN BESS
Elizabeth I (ruled 1558–1603) rebuilt England after it had been weakened by the rule of her father, King Henry VIII.

Empire builders

An empire is a collection of countries under one ruler. The Roman Empire flourished under its first emperor, Augustus (63 B.C.–A.D. 14), and at its peak stretched from Spain to Mesopotamia (modern-day Iraq). The western part of Rome's empire crumbled in the 400s, but in A.D. 800 Charlemagne of France revived it as the Holy Roman empire, turning Western Europe into a Christian superstate.

The Mughal emperors ruled much of India from the 1525 invasion by Babur until the death of Muhammad Shah in 1748. Of all the Mughals, Akbar was the greatest. Tolerant of all religions and a skilled administrator, he earned the title "Guardian of Mankind."

LOOK EAST
Genghis Khan (1162–1227) built one of the largest-ever empires. It covered Asia from the Black Sea east to China. Though cruel, he was a skillful leader of the Mongols. His descendant Babur (1483–1530) ruled northern India.

FACTS AND FIGURES

The Soviet Union broke up in the late 1980s under the moderate leadership of Mikhail Gorbachev.

Sargon of Akkad, an empire builder in Mesopotamia (modern-day Iraq), ruled 55 years until he died in 2279 B.C.

Haile Selassie, emperor of Ethiopia (1930–1974), is seen as a black messiah by the Rastafarian religious group.

General Charles de Gaulle, a brave soldier and patriot, was president of the French Fifth Republic from 1959–1969.

Religious leaders

Religious leaders are dedicated to promoting and preserving their faith. Constantine, the first Roman emperor to become a Christian, built churches across his mighty empire during his rule in the 4th century A.D. Saladin (1137–1193) was a Muslim sultan of Yemen, Syria, Palestine, and Egypt. He fought off Christian crusaders and captured Jerusalem in 1187. In Tibet in central Asia spiritual leaders known as Dalai Lamas have been the guiding force behind Buddhism since the 1390s.

HOLY MEN
For more than one thousand years the Roman Catholic Church has appointed spiritual leaders called popes.

HOW WISE
Little is known about Lao Tzu, a wise man living in China 2,500 years ago. He was the first philosopher of Taoism, a calm, thoughtful way of life in which you shun the world and commune with nature.

HIGH IDEALS
Buddhism spread widely under the reign of Asoka, an emperor of India during the 3rd century B.C. After winning a war he turned away from fighting. He had Buddhist truths carved on pillars and rocks in India and other lands.

Moses, who led the Jews out of Egyptian slavery in 1290 B.C., is believed to be the father of Judaism and its greatest prophet.

Military leaders

Leaders rely on a strong, loyal army. In the past they usually marched with their troops. Alexander the Great won dozens of military victories. At the time of his death in 323 B.C., aged 32, this Macedonian king held all of the lands from Greece to India. A century later the Carthaginian general Hannibal (247–181 B.C.) took his army over the Alps into Italy. He fought the Romans, but the inferior-sized army finally let him down. The French emperor Napoleon Bonaparte waged war across Europe from 1800–1815. Though ultimately in vain, he won many victories, usually by massing his troops in one brutal attack. Napoleon's writings on war were carried by Confederate General Thomas "Stonewall" Jackson, a brilliant military planner in the 1861– 1865 American Civil War.

Prussian soldier Karl von Clausewitz wrote *On War* (1832–1837), a military strategy guide in which he recommended "total war."

ALEXANDER THE GREAT
Leading his first battle at the age of 16, Alexander later conquered Persia (modern-day Iran) at the head of an army of more than 35,000 men.

THE WARRIOR
Napoleon Bonaparte was finally defeated at Waterloo in 1815 but not before he had revolutionized the art of troop warfare.

HEROES

A hero is someone who inspires people through their bravery, dedication, or leadership. Through their example they can give others the courage to take a stand and can even change the course of history.

TIME OF CHANGE
John Brown attacked supporters of slavery in the U.S. His execution in 1859 inspired others to bring an end to slavery.

Inspiring lives

When the steamship *Forfarshire* sank off the coast of England in 1838, nine passengers were stranded on the rocks. Despite the storm, a lighthouse keeper's daughter named Grace Darling rowed out to save them.

Another popular heroine is Josephine Baker. Born poor, she danced and sang in the theaters of Paris in the 1920s and became the first black star in entertainment. Some people never give up, however hard life is. In the 1940s Anne Frank and her family, who were Jewish, lived in an attic in Amsterdam for two years to hide from the German Nazis. Eventually they were found and taken to a prison camp, but Anne's diary of their terrible ordeal survived.

SAINT JOAN
Joan of Arc believed that she was acting on God's orders. Burned to death in 1431, she was made a saint in 1920.

Spirit of resistance

Many people who resist cruel governments or their country's enemies become heroes. In 1428 a peasant girl called Joan of Arc inspired the weary French soldiers and led them to victory against the invading English army. Later the invaders came back for Joan and killed her, but to this day she is remembered as a national heroine. Another national hero was the soldier Giuseppe Garibaldi who, in the 1830s–1870s, inspired his fellow Italians to fight against French and Austrian rule. Today Aung San Suu Kyi is leading a nonviolent struggle against the military rulers of Myanmar (Burma) in Southeast Asia to win more freedom for her people.

CHAMPION OF THE SIOUX
Chief Tatanka Iyotake (Sitting Bull) rallied the Sioux tribes against invading U.S. troops in 1876, but in the end his men were starved into surrendering

THE LIBERATOR
In 1819–1825 Simón Bolívar freed Colombia, his native Venezuela, Ecuador, Peru, and Bolivia after three centuries of Spanish rule in South America.

Scotland's hero William Wallace and his outnumbered warriors defeated th English army at the Battle of Stirling Bridge in 1297.

T. E. LAWRENCE
During World War I (1914–1918) English soldier Thomas E. Lawrence planned an Arab revolt against Turkey, Germany's ally at the time. Dressed as an Arab, he staged daring raids on enemy positions in Arabia.

Deeds of kindness

It is human nature to help people in need. A pioneer of social work was Irish-born Dr. Thomas Barnardo. He established homes for orphans in the slums of 19th-century English cities. In 1985 Irish singer Bob Geldof gathered many musicians for Live Aid—two rock concerts, staged in England and the United States, that were shown live on TV worldwide. Live Aid raised millions of dollars to go toward feeding starving victims of the famine in Ethiopia.

In Mexico today LIGA is an organization that sends volunteer doctors and nurses to treat the poor. Its "flying doctors" use light aircraft to reach even remote villages in the forests.

MOTHER TERESA
Born Agnes Bojaxhiu in Macedonia in 1910, she gave help to the poor and sick in India until her death in 1997.

FACTS AND FIGURES

Chief Vercingetorix rallied the Gauls to resist the Roman troops of Julius Caesar until he was captured in 52 B.C.

The German pastor Dietrich Bonhoeffer bravely criticized the Nazis' racist policies. In 1945 they murdered him.

English spy Violet Szabo went behind enemy lines in World War II and sent back coded messages disguised as poetry.

In 1980 Lech Walesa founded the labor union Solidarity to protect workers' rights in Communist Poland.

LADY OF THE LAMP
Florence Nightingale tended to wounded soldiers and, in London in 1860, set up the first school for nurses.

BIRTH OF THE RED CROSS
After tending to war wounded in 1859 Switzerland's Jean-Henri Dunant planned what would become the International Red Cross, a relief agency.

St. Francis of Assisi, Italy, founded the Franciscan order in 1209. He was kind not only to people but also to animals.

Unsung heroes

Every day there are countless examples of heroism that we do not hear about. Unsung heroes include the nurses and doctors who save lives in hospitals, police officers who put their lives in danger while fighting crime, and the firefighters and paramedics who rescue people after disasters. Coast Guard crews go out to sea in howling storms to rescue ships in trouble. On icy peaks mountain rescue teams risk danger searching for lost climbers.

INTO THE INFERNO
Firefighters regularly risk their lives to put out blazes like this, and ambulance workers know that every second counts as they rush the injured to hospitals.

THE ULTIMATE SACRIFICE
Even when it seems wrong to fight, soldiers have a job to do— a deadly one. This is part of a memorial to U.S. casualties in the 1965–1973 Vietnam War.

PHILOSOPHIES AND RELIGIONS

Philosophy is the pursuit of wisdom and knowledge. A religion is a system of belief in one god or more or in a spiritual force. Philosophies and religions can help us make sense of our often confusing world.

Great thinkers

Philosophers are people who think hard about life and offer wise ideas that can make sense of it all. Born in Athens around 470 B.C., Socrates was a great talker. For him, conversation was a path to wisdom. One of his best pupils, Plato, studied the difference between the ideas in our minds and what we can actually see. Another Greek, Aristotle, believed in logical thinking. In 18th-century Germany, Immanuel Kant wrote about what people believe and how they make decisions. He lived during Europe's Enlightenment, a time when people valued reason and scientific thought. Many modern thinkers write about human nature, freedom, and justice.

SUMMIT MEETING
In 508 B.C. democracy came to Athens. The people of the city met on Pnyx Hill to debate important issues.

Confucius, born in China in 551 B.C., said that everyone can shape their own destiny. His teachings have inspired millions in Asia.

UNPOPULAR PRESS
In France in 1751–1772 Denis Diderot helped publish an encyclopedia full of new ideas that upset both church and state.

FACTS AND FIGURES

In 12th-century Spain, Islamic scholar Averroës interpreted the works of Greek thinkers Plato and Aristotle.

The works of French writer Simone de Beauvoir (1908–1986) combine her interests in feminism and philosophy.

In his book *The Republic* (360 B.C.) Greek philosopher Plato dreamed up a perfect land of freedom and fairness.

French historian Alexis de Tocqueville wrote *Democracy in America* (1835–1840), a study of U.S. politics.

SIGMUND FREUD
This Austrian, who died in 1939, suggested that our dreams and other hidden thoughts affect how we act.

Big political ideas

Many countries use a political plan, refined in ancient Greece, called democracy. In a democracy people can vote for change. In the 1900s Scotland's Adam Smith said that government should let businesses run the economy. This is called capitalism, and it is used in many democracies. German thinker Karl Marx attacked capitalism. If businesses are free, he said, their workers suffer—why not make all people equal? Russia's Vladimir Lenin developed his idea, calling it communism or socialism. It failed in the Soviet Union but lives on in China, Cuba, and North Korea.

BALLOT BOX
In a democracy the people vote for their leader of choice. During an election the votes are placed in boxes like this.

IMAGINE . . .

German political thinker Karl Marx looked forward to the day when the working class earned a fair wage and all people were equal. That day hasn't arrived, but Marxism—his philosophy—still has followers.

Russia became the world's first Communist state, the Soviet Union, or U.S.S.R., after the 1917 Revolution. The Union ended in 1991.

Myths

Myths are mixtures of stories, beliefs, and traditions. They include fairy tales, fables, and legends. Creation myths are about human origins. The ancient Babylonians thought people were the offspring of a marriage between earth and sky, created from a mixture of clay and blood. The North American Zuni believed we rose up from the depths of the world. The complex mythology of the ancient Greeks included hundreds of legends and epic poems about their gods and heroes.

Tuesday, Wednesday, Thursday, and Friday are named after old Germanic or Norse gods: Tiw, Wodin, Thor, and Frigga.

ACCORDING TO LEGEND . . .
The Norse gods bound the ferocious wolf Fenrir with chains made from a woman's beard, a cat's footsteps, and a fish's breath.

PROTEST MAN
In 1517 Germany's Martin Luther wrote an attack on corruption in the church. This triggered the Reformation, a wave of social change in Europe, as well as a new branch of Christianity known as Protestantism.

World religions

There are many religions in the world today. Judaism was founded in the Holy Land 3,500 years ago. Jews believe they are the chosen people of Jehovah (God). Christianity grew out of Judaism. Christians follow the teachings of Jesus Christ, who lived in the Middle East 2,000 years ago. They say he was the Son of God, sent as a sacrifice to save the human race from punishment for their sins. The main branches of Christianity are Roman Catholicism, Eastern Orthodoxy, and Protestantism. Islam is a faith based on the life of the holy Prophet Mohammed (b. A.D. 570). Its followers, called Muslims, believe Allah (God) dictated his teachings to Mohammed.

Hinduism is an ancient religion from India. It has no founder, single teacher, or prophets. Instead Hindus believe in a universal soul known as Brahman. They worship many gods such as Krishna and Shiva. In the religion of Buddhism there are no gods to worship. Buddhists study and meditate to gain personal spiritual development.

Animism is the name given to primitive religions in which followers see spiritual power in living things and objects.

GANESH
An image of this elephant-headed god, offspring of the great god Shiva, can often be seen over the doorways of Hindu temples. Another animal god worshiped in Hinduism includes Hanuman, a heroic monkey.

MARY, MOTHER OF JESUS
In Christianity, especially in the Roman Catholic faith, the Virgin Mary is revered. She symbolizes absolute purity, as well as total obedience to God's command.

SHOFAR
This musical instrument, made from a ram's horn, is sounded on Rosh Hashanah and other Jewish holy days.

STATE OF ENLIGHTENMENT
Buddhist statues look peaceful. Buddhists meditate in order to achieve nirvana—a state of the highest peace and perfection.

LITERATURE

The earliest writings were on stone and clay, and only a few people could read them. Now we write books on every subject imaginable for the enjoyment of millions of readers.

READ ON!
A new printing press made in the 1450s by Johannas Gutenberg of Germany was the start of affordable books for all. His first printing was a bible. This title is the biggest seller ever, with billions of copies in over 2,000 languages.

In the beginning

Literature began 30,000 years ago when early Stone-Age people first drew pictures in caves to tell stories. From simple pictures called pictograms, languages grew. Once people learned to tell stories they added excitement, plots, and colorful description. Great tales like the *Iliad* and *Odyssey*, written by Homer in Greece in the 700s B.C., are epics—tales full of wars, heroic deeds, long journeys, and often with a supernatural element. Homer's works inspired Virgil, who wrote in Rome 700 years later. Virgil's own unfinished epic, the *Aeneid*, recounts Rome's history. Luckily for us, the emperor refused Virgil's dying wish that the epic be burned. In China from the 500s B.C. spiritual thinkers, such as Confucius and Lao-tsu, put their ideas on paper. Religion took up most writers' time until the Middle Ages. In 1387 the Englishman Geoffrey Chaucer began writing the *Canterbury Tales*, which looked at how people really lived, as well as how they should live.

In 1824 Frenchman Louis Braille designed braille—an "alphabet" of raised dots on paper enabling blind people to "feel" words.

BAYEUX TAPESTRY
Woven in 1067–1077, this 230 ft. length of embroidery uses pictures to tell the story of the Norman conquest of Great Britain in 1066. It is full of battle scenes.

Strong words

Words are powerful, and they can cause trouble. Aleksandr Solzhenitsyn (b. 1918) was exiled from the Soviet Union for writing about life in Siberian labor camps. Some authors use satire, a fierce type of humor, to attack people or ideas. Great satirists from past centuries include Frenchman François Rabelais (1494–1553) and Irish-born Jonathan Swift (1667–1745). *Catch-22* (1961), a satirical novel by American writer Joseph Heller, attacked the lunacy of war.

GIANT TALE
Gulliver's Travels (1726) by Jonathan Swift is a satirical novel. Not just a good story, it also pokes fun at our weaker natures.

JOURNEYMAN
In *The Divine Comedy* by Italian Dante Alighieri (1265–1321) a man journeys through hell, purgatory, and heaven.

Poetry

Words in poetry are chosen as much for their sound as for their meaning. In 1817 English poet John Keats wrote that poetry should "lift the thoughts of man." Poems can vary greatly in length. The Indian epic *Mahabharata* has almost 200,000 lines, while a Japanese haiku has only three. American poet Emily Dickinson (1830–1886) wrote brief, intense verses. Poetry can be funny, too. English poet Edward Lear (1812–1888) wrote limericks (funny poems) for children, as did the American writer Ogden Nash (1902–1971).

The first "books" were passed around on clay tablets; paper was invented by the Chinese in A.D. 105.

Books for the young

The first children's books, such as the 15th-century *Babees' Book*, were stern lectures on how to be good, but children's literature has moved on since then. Creators of lovable animal characters include A. A. Milne (Winnie-the-Pooh), Beatrix Potter (Peter Rabbit and others), and Jean de Brunhoff (Babar, the Little Elephant). English writers J. R. R. Tolkien and C. S. Lewis conjured up magical kingdoms—one created Middle Earth, the other, Narnia. The books of New York writer and illustrator Maurice Sendak include *Where the Wild Things Are* (1963). Harry Potter, J. K. Rowling's wizard boy, has cast a spell over both children and adults since he first appeared in 1997.

HANS UP
Born into poverty in 1805, Hans Christian Andersen of Denmark won fame with his charming, and often sad, fairy tales.

ANIMAL MAGIC
Alice's Adventures in Wonderland (1865) is a dreamlike tale by Lewis Carroll about an inquisitive little girl.

COME IN!
The witch tempts Hansel and Gretel—one of the tales (1812–1822) by the German brothers Wilhelm and Jacob Grimm.

FANTASTIC VOYAGE
Frenchman Jules Verne (1828–1905) launched science-fiction writing with tales of undersea and space exploration.

The novel

A good novel has an involving plot and detailed characters. One of the most popular novels of all time is *Don Quixote*, a knight's tale by the Spanish writer Miguel de Cervantes in 1605–1615. Novels can reveal what life was like at the time of writing. *Tom Jones* (1749) by Henry Fielding is like a snapshot of England in the 1900s. Charles Dickens put 19th-century realism in his bittersweet novels set in poorhouses and slums. Stories by Honoré de Balzac, who died in 1850, tell us about French society. By the mid-1900s genre novels—stories with themes such as horror or crime—were popular. Today we have books by international authors such as Nigerian Chinua Achebe, Canadian Margaret Atwood, and V. S. Naipaul from Trinidad (who won the Nobel Prize for Literature in 2001).

George Eliot (Mary Ann Evans), Jane Austen, and the three Brontë sisters wrote some of the best English novels of the 1800s.

NOBEL PRIZEWINNER, 1982
Colombian Gabriel García Márquez writes stories that are both magical and real—such as *One Hundred Years of Solitude* (1967).

FACTS AND FIGURES

Italy's Petrarch (1304–1374) wrote beautiful poems to Laura, a woman he loved from a distance for 50 years.

French poet Victor Hugo (1802–1885) also wrote fine novels—such as *Notre-Dame de Paris* and *Les Misérables*.

American-born T. S. Eliot pioneered modern poetry with works such as *The Waste Land* (1922).

Audio books aren't just a fun way to enjoy stories—they improve our concentration and listening skills.

MOVING MAN
The tales of Charles Dickens (1812–1870) affected readers so deeply that the government changed English laws to improve life for society's outcasts. This scene is from the novel *David Copperfield* (1849–1850).

PERFORMING ARTS

People enjoy dressing up and performing, and the art of turning words and music into public shows has been with us for over 25 centuries.

OH, WHAT A CIRCUS
Roman plays were mostly based on ancient Greek classics, and actors usually sang and wore masks.

Opening act

In the 400s–500s B.C. Greek playwrights like Euripides, Sophocles, and Aristophanes entertained Athenians with stories about the gods. Some were tragedies, and others were comedies. Drama was very popular in ancient Rome—but so were battling gladiators and hungry lions!

Europe's greatest playwright is William Shakespeare (1564–1616). Like the Greeks he wrote tragedies, such as *Hamlet*, and comedies, such as *Twelfth Night*. Great French humorists include Molière (1622–1673), who even poked fun at the church.

SUN KING
In 1653 France's Louis XIV danced in a ballet as the sun god Apollo. He was a cultured king and lover of the arts.

ROUND UP
From 1599 Shakespeare's plays were staged in London's Globe Theater. Closed by Puritans in 1642 and pulled down in 1644, the Globe was rebuilt 350 years later. It now holds regular Shakespeare seasons.

Great actors

Some actors became as famous as the characters they played. In England, David Garrick (1717–1779) and Laurence Olivier (1907–1989) specialized in roles from Shakespeare. So did German actor Ludwig Devrient (1784–1832), head of a family of famous actors.

Polus of ancient Greece was a dedicated actor. To inspire grief in the tragedy *Electra* he carried the real ashes of his dead son!

Behind top actors are great directors. In the early 1900s in Russia, Konstantin Stanislavsky coached actors for the subtle dialogues in plays by Anton Chekhov. Some Hollywood actors, such as Marlon Brando and Sidney Poitier, later used Stanislavsky's "method," which was taught to them by New York director Lee Strasberg.

STAGE STARS
Here are Laurence Olivier and Vivien Leigh as Shakespeare's *Anthony and Cleopatra*. On the stage for much of the 1900s, Olivier also starred in films of Shakespeare's plays like *Hamlet* and *Henry V*.

DAZZLING!
This amazing costume was made for a Paris production of *The Firebird*, a ballet by Michel Fokine and Igor Stravinsky, in 1910. The show, performed by Sergei Diaghilev's Ballets Russes (Russian ballet), was a success.

Arthur Miller's play *The Crucible* is about witch-hunts in the 1800s, but it can also be read as an attack on American society in the 1950s.

Opera

Operas are plays set to music and often sung in Italian or German. Famous Italian operas include *Norma* (1831) by Vincenzo Bellini, *La Traviata* (1853) and *Aïda* (1871) by Giuseppe Verdi, and *La Bohème* (1896) by Giacomo Puccini. With lavish sets, huge casts, and the best singers, operas can be expensive. But opera has many popular forms. "Music hall," or vaudeville (slapstick and singing), boomed in the 1930s–1950s. Rock opera has produced classic hits such as *Cats*. Even opera has its lighter side. Austria's Wolfgang Mozart mixed *opera buffa* (comic opera) with *opera seria* (serious opera) in *The Marriage of Figaro* (1786) and other works. In Victorian England the witty lyrics of William Gilbert were set to Arthur Sullivan's catchy music in operettas—light operas with a romantic plot—like *Pirates of Penzance* (1879).

A NIGHT AT THE OPERA
A scene unfolds at the Opéra in Paris, 1789. Other famous opera venues include La Scala in Milan, Italy, and the Metropolitan in New York City.

ROLLIN' STOCK
All of the actors wear roller skates in *Starlight Express* (1984), a musical by Englishman Andrew Lloyd Webber.

The expressive soprano voice of American Maria Callas (1923–1977) made her one of the most famous of all opera divas.

Mime and dance

Mime is silent acting using actions and facial expressions to show emotion. It has been performed for nearly 2,500 years since the Greek Classical period. Comedy is just as old. British pantomimes—fairy tales such as *Cinderella* that use comedy and audience participation—use styles of humor developed in the 1700s by the Italian Commedia dell'Arte touring companies.

Ballet is graceful, theatrical dancing set to music. It first flourished in the French royal courts of the late 1600–1700s. Russian Peter Tchaikovsky wrote favorites such as *Swan Lake* (1877), *The Sleeping Beauty* (1890), and *The Nutcracker* (1892).

HIGH POINT
Ballerinas dance *en pointe* (on tiptoe). One of the first to perfect this was Swedish-born Maria Taglioni in 1832.

KABUKI
Japanese Kabuki theater began in the 1600s. It uses singing, dancing, and comedy. Make up and fancy wigs are worn to express personality.

FACTS AND FIGURES

In some tribal cultures dance is a way of remembering the past instead of writing it down. Try that at school!

Irish-born Samuel Beckett is best known for *Waiting for Godot* (1952), a play in which very little happens.

In 1986 Nigerian playwright Wole Soyinka won the Nobel Prize for Literature—the first black African to do so.

American Philip Glass writes operas in a "minimalist" style—the music has few notes but still sounds complicated.

VISUAL ARTS

Artists use their skills and unique vision to show us what the world looks like through their eyes. Photographers, craftspeople, and designers have also left their own personal impacts.

PICTURES OF CREATION
Australian Aborigines believe the world was made in "Dreamtime," an ancient era. This is shown in their early rock paintings.

A window on the world

Art enables us to show others how we look at life. Early humans drew mythical subjects and hunting scenes on cave walls. Painters of medieval Europe painted formal pictures of Bible scenes. In the 1300s the work of the Italian painter Giotto di Bondone introduced a new style known as the Renaissance. His sculptures and frescoes (paintings on wet plaster) featured more realistic figures. The greatest Renaissance artist was the Italian sculptor, architect, and painter Michelangelo.

The *Mona Lisa* (1503–1536) by Italian Leonardo da Vinci is the world's most famous portrait, due to its female subject's secretive smile.

Another upheaval came in the 1800s when Claude Monet, Edouard Manet, and other French artists began painting outside. Their work, known as Impressionism, upset traditional artists, but it would later encourage early 20th-century artists like Russian Wassily Kandinsky. He was one of the new abstract painters, showing patterns and shapes instead of "real" people or places.

BIG SPLASH
Katsushika Hokusai was a Japanese painter and engraver. He used a free and graceful but also stylized art form. In the 1820s Hokusai made a woodcut print, now very famous, called *The Great Wave at Kanagawa*.

GODDESS
Italian Sandro Botticelli painted *The Birth of Venus* around 1485. It shows godly beauty entering the human world.

Modern trail-blazers

Modern art constantly challenges our ideas about beauty. Spain's Pablo Picasso was the most famous painter of the 1900s. Depicting people in bizarre, twisted shapes, his art was full of emotion. Another Spanish artist, Salvador Dalí, painted surprising images in a style called Surrealism. In the United States, Jackson Pollock made chaotic abstract paintings. He would drip or flick paint onto a canvas stuck to the floor. In recent years English artist Damien Hirst became well-known using pickled animals and other strange pieces of art.

The huge artworks of Bulgarian-born Christo include city buildings and bridges wrapped in paper or plastic.

WHAT IS IT WORTH?
Pablo Picasso's work changes hands for lots of money. In 1997 one of his portraits sold for $48 million!

An eye for design

Design is the creative use of shapes, images, patterns, colors, or text to create a picture or object. Many designers are also artists. For example, in 1890s Paris Alphonse Mucha created posters in a lavish style called Art Nouveau—"new art." One of the most important schools of modern design was the Bauhaus, founded in Germany in 1919. Paul Klee, Johannes Itten, and other artist-designers taught subjects ranging from pottery and stained glass to woodwork. Many brought what they learned to the United States, including the architects Walter Gropius and Ludwig Mies van der Rohe. Already making his name in America was Paul Rand. He designed everything from book covers to posters and textiles.

THROUGH THE MIND'S EYE
German artist and design teacher Paul Klee shows creative use of shape, line, and color in *Caprice in February* (1939).

Antony Gormley's giant statue *Angel of the North* (1998) stands in a field in the north of England. Its outspread wings span 177 ft.

Sculptors

Early sculptures were often statues of great people or gods. Michelangelo carved *David*, a statue that became a symbol for his hometown of Florence. Auguste Rodin (1840–1917) was France's most expressive sculptor. In the 1900s England's Henry Moore created lumpy figures in stone and bronze. Swiss sculptor Alberto Giacometti made thin, sad-looking portraits. Another Swiss, Jean Tinguely, created mechanical sculptures that could draw pictures or play music!

Grinling Gibbons (1648–1721) carved detailed wood and stone decorations in England's royal palaces and great churches.

FACTS AND FIGURES

The oldest known pieces of art—little statues and carvings of animals—are around 30,000 years old.

Byzantine art began in the eastern Roman empire in A.D. 330 when the city of Constantinople was founded.

Impressionist art is named after an 1872 painting by Claude Monet called *Impression: Sunrise.*

In 1888 Dutchman Vincent van Gogh painted a series of sunflowers. They now sell for millions of dollars.

TURNED TO STONE
Italian Renaissance sculptors made their statues look almost real. Here Michelangelo adds the finishing touches to a statue of Moses in 1513.

Creative crafts

Good craftsmanship is respected all over the world. Some of the best porcelain, for example, is from China, notably from the Ming Dynasty (1368–1644). In the 1800s Russian jeweler Karl Fabergé crafted treasures, like the Easter eggs made for Csar Alexander III's family. In France, René Lalique made fine jewelry and glass perfume bottles. Today collectors pay large amounts for the richly colored Art Deco teacups and milk jugs of Clarice Cliff.

WINGS OF DESIRE
This bird brooch, crafted from jewels set in gold, is a treasure from the Ostrogoth empire, which covered northern Europe during the A.D. 200s–500s.

FISH DISH
The pottery of ancient Greece shows scenes from mythology or daily life, like this fisherman setting his nets.

MOVIES

In their history of just over 100 years movies have become one of the most popular art forms. Movie industries have sprung up worldwide, and everyone has their own movie favorites.

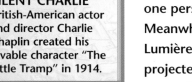 ## Making images move

In 1888 French-born Augustin le Prince shot the first movie. It was silent since the technology to produce sound had not been developed. One year later American inventor Thomas Edison and his British assistant, William Dickson, made a new camera and viewer—but only one person could watch the film at a time. Meanwhile, in France, Auguste and Louis Lumière invented the *Cinématographe*, a camera that projected the film onto a screen for large audiences. The Lumières's first movie theater opened in 1895. Charles Pathé then improved their inventions, and by 1918 more than half of all movies made were shot on Pathé cameras.

The first successful "talkie," or film with sound, was *The Jazz Singer* (1927), directed by Alan Crosland and starring Al Jolson.

SILENT CHARLIE
British-American actor and director Charlie Chaplin created his lovable character "The Little Tramp" in 1914.

Hollywood

Hollywood, California is the home of American moviemaking. In its early years each film studio had its own set of actors. By 1919 Charlie Chaplin was so successful that no studio could afford him so he founded his own—United Artists. It soon joined the ranks of other giant studios, including Paramount, MGM, 20th Century–Fox, and RKO. Today movie stars can work with any studio they choose.

But stars may stick to certain roles—John Wayne made westerns, while Gene Kelly danced in musicals and Bette Davis played fiery characters. Others have achieved fame as child stars, including Shirley Temple, Macaulay Culkin, Anna Paquin, and Haley Joel Osment. Top African-American stars include Eddie Murphy, Will Smith, Samuel L. Jackson, and Whoopie Goldberg.

TOUGH GUY AND HIS GAL
Humphrey Bogart and his wife Lauren Bacall made great films together—such as the gangster movie, *The Big Sleep* (1946).

BIG SMILE
Julia Roberts won a Golden Globe award and an Oscar in 2001 for her role in *Erin Brockovich*. Her other movie successes include *Notting Hill* (1999), *Flatliners* (1990), *Pretty Woman* (also 1990), and *Mystic PIzza* (1988).

ICY GLAMOUR
German-born actress Marlene Dietrich acted sultry and sophisticated in such movies as *The Blue Angel* (1930).

SUPERMODEL
Today's movies use digital effects, but vintage monster movies, such as *King Kong* (1933), used working models. Dinosaurs, such as this *T. rex*, prowled around in *The Land that Time Forgot* (1975) and *Jurassic Park* (1993).

In the director's chair

The overall feel of a movie is created by the director. France's Georges Méliès was one of the first directors. His *Trip to the Moon* (1902) is full of special effects and humor. American director D. W. Griffith

Crouching Tiger, Hidden Dragon (2000), a Chinese-language film by Ang Lee, won four Oscars at the 73rd Academy Awards.

"BOLLYWOOD"—CINEMA OF INDIA
India's movie industry releases more feature-length movies per year than any other country, peaking in 1990 at 948 movies.

pioneered new techniques, like the use of close-ups. But his racist movies, such as *The Birth of a Nation* (1915), show us that a director can abuse his power and send negative as well as positive messages. *Potemkin* (1925), directed by Sergei Eisenstein, sent a strong political message celebrating the Russian Revolution of 1905.

Every director has a unique style. Swedish-born Ingmar Bergman made bleak, intense films; Italian Federico Fellini created dreamlike scenes. French "New Wave" directors, like Louis Malle and François Truffaut, used simple sets to escape the glossy feel of commercial movies. John Ford shot westerns and other action movies.

ALFRED HITCHCOCK
The British-born king of thriller movies directs Grace Kelly and James Stewart in *Rear Window* (1954), in which a man suspects his neighbor of murder.

Getting animated

To animate means "to bring to life," which is exactly what cartoonists do to their characters. Walt Disney's Mickey Mouse first amazed audiences in *Steamboat Willie* (1928), and *Snow White and the Seven Dwarfs* (1937) was the first in a long line of feature-length Disney cartoons.

"Stop motion" involves movable models. U.S. modeler Ray Harryhausen used the technique to animate model skeletons in *Jason and the Argonauts* (1963). More recently Wallace and Gromit won awards for their British animator, Nick Park. Some animations, such as *Toy Story* (1995) and *Final Fantasy: The Spirits Within* (2001), were made completely on computers.

Cartoonist Walt Disney holds the record for the most Oscar nominations—64. Disney actually won 26 Oscars during his lifetime.

FACTS AND FIGURES

Ben-Hur (1959) and *Titanic* (1997) each won a record 11 Oscars. *Titanic* had received 14 nominations.

Katharine Hepburn won four Best Actress Oscars. Seven actors, including Tom Hanks, have won Best Actor twice.

India's finest director was Satyajit Ray. His films include *The Song of the Road* (1955) and *The Lonely Wife* (1964).

New Zealand director Jane Campion won awards at the Cannes Film Festival in France for *The Piano* (1994).

Iran produces 70–80 movies a year. Its best-known directors include Majid Majidi, Abbas Kiarostami, and Jafar Panahi.

MUSIC

Early civilizations created music as an offering to their gods. Today choirs still sing hymns, but most music is made for our own enjoyment—and for success in the charts!

SAINTLY MUSE
This is St. Cecilia, the Roman patron saint of music. She is frequently depicted playing a small organ.

SITAR
It can take a lifetime to master the sitar. A type of lute, it features in folk and dance music of northern India. The Beatles and other 1960s pop groups used the sitar to give their songs an eastern sound.

To the glory of God

Music was probably first used to please the gods. Christian monks began to write down music in the 800s, and choirs started to sing polyphonic ("lots of voices") hymns. Later the organ was added. Modern Christian choirs still sing psalms, song poems from the Old Testament of the Bible. Catholic choirs perform formal musical settings of the mass. The choirs of Baptist churches sing gospel songs and spirituals, and the congregation is encouraged to join in.

Qawwali is a type of religious music popular with Sufi Muslims. Its finest singer was Nusrat Fateh Ali Khan (1948–1997).

STREET PARTY
A steel drum band is the heart and soul of Caribbean carnivals. Steel drums, first played on the island of Trinidad, are made from old shipping containers.

Classical music

The most popular works of European classical music date from the 1600s–1800s and are played by an orchestra—a group of musicians who play different instruments. In Germany, Johann Sebastian Bach composed church music in the extravagant baroque style. Ludwig van Beethoven later wrote stirring symphonies and gentle pieces for the piano. In Austria, Wolfgang Amadeus Mozart wrote more than 600 delicate pieces. In the early 1900s modern composers got rid of the order and control of classical music. The experimental music of American Arnold Schoenberg and Russian Igor Stravinsky can sound harsh or ugly to some ears but exciting to others.

ROMANTIC
Edward Elgar (1857–1934) rekindled English classical music with works like the *Enigma Variations* (1896).

CHILD STAR
Mozart (1756–1791) began writing music at five years old. To show him off, his father toured him through Europe.

French composer Claude Debussy (1862–1918) was often inspired by art. "I love pictures," he once said, "almost as much as music itself."

Jazz

Jazz was born in the U.S. South in the 1890s from a mixture of brass band music, African rhythms, and slaves' work songs. Louis Armstrong began playing his trumpet for bandleader Joe "King" Oliver in New Orleans in the 1920s. He was one of the first soloists. Other great soloists have been John Coltrane and Coleman Hawkins (saxophone), Miles Davis and Dizzy Gillespie (trumpet), Art Tatum (piano), and Gene Krupa (drums). The best players can improvise—they make up the music as they play!

THE DUKE
Edward Kennedy "Duke" Ellington (1899–1974) led a great jazz band and wrote music for movies, opera, and theater.

FACTS AND FIGURES

Archaeologists have found a flute almost 80,000 years old in Slovenia. It plays "do-re-mi" like a modern instrument.

Ludwig van Beethoven began composing his *Mass in D* after he had been suffering from bouts of deafness for 18 years.

U.S. composer John Cage's *4'33"* is a four-minute, 33-second period of silence to be "played" by a pianist.

TOP BRASS
A magnificent trumpet soloist, Louis Armstrong (1901–1971) was also a fine singer with a trademark gravelly voice.

SPIN CYCLE
German-born Emile Berliner invented flat records in 1887 using glass, zinc, and rubber. Columbia Records introduced the 33.3rpm vinyl LP in 1948.

MESSAGE IN MUSIC
The lyrics in Bob Dylan's folk-inspired songs are just as important as the music. Here he performs with fellow American musician Joan Baez.

Going pop

The roots of pop ("popular") music are in blues and the jazzy music played in hot, smoky nightclubs, originally by African-American musicians. In the 1950s Little Richard, Elvis Presley, and Buddy Holly were the first U.S. rock 'n' roll stars. The Beatles, who followed them, wrote highly original songs. The Rolling Stones modeled themselves on American blues singers before finding their own style. Since the early years there have been endless changes to the character of pop—from the sunny surf sound of the Beach Boys, the urban soul of Motown, the stomp of disco, and the angry yell of punk to the dance beats of house, drum 'n' bass, and techno.

Paul McCartney and John Lennon, from The Beatles, are credited as joint songwriters on 23 No. 1 singles in the U.S. (25 in Great Britain).

QUEEN OF POP
Ex-Mouseketeer Britney Spears was only 17 years old when her debut album, . . . *Baby One More Time* (1999), entered the U.S. charts at No. 1. Her second, *Oops! . . . I Did It Again* (2000), also sold by the millions.

29

UNIVERSAL LAWS

Science is about understanding nature—from tiny particles to outer space. The more we know, the more we see that everything is ruled by universal laws.

DON'T TRY THIS AT HOME!
In 1752 American Benjamin Franklin flew a kite in a storm to prove that a lightning strike was an electrical discharge. He later invented the lightning rod.

The scientific work of people such as James Maxwell and Albert Einstein has enabled us to explore outer space.

Forces of nature

When Italian Galileo Galilei started testing his ideas about gravity in the 1580s, he invented the modern scientific technique. Englishman Isaac Newton, born in 1642, studied gravity too. He saw that falling objects obey the laws of physics that apply to everything. His laws dominated science for over 200 years. Later German-born Albert Einstein saw that some things, such as the speed of light, don't obey Newton's laws. So in 1905 he produced new rules—the theory of relativity—that can be used to predict the behavior of the entire universe.

RAINBOW
In 1666 Isaac Newton used a prism to prove that "white" light contains the full range of colors.

FACTS AND FIGURES

The main difference between light and other electromagnetic waves is that we can see light.

Light travels an incredible 186,000 mph—the equivalent of seven times around the world—in a second!

Scientists say the universe was created 12 billion years ago in a huge blast—the "Big Bang"—and is still expanding.

As early as 1600 William Gilbert, the doctor of Queen Elizabeth I of England, suggested (correctly) that Earth is a giant magnet.

What is light?

Back in Newton's day Dutch astronomer Christiaan Huygens proposed that light is a rippling wave traveling through space. Much later, in the 1840s, English scientist Michael Faraday suggested that Earth hangs in a web of radiating electrical and magnetic forces and that light is a visible vibration of these forces. In the 1860s the idea was used by James Clerk Maxwell. He proved that electricity, light, and magnetism are all part of one force called electromagnetic radiation. He predicted other types of electromagnetic radiation, including the radio waves and microwaves that activate our televisions and cell phones.

POSITIVE MAN
It was Victorian scientist Michael Faraday's idea that Earth hangs in a huge field of magnetic and electrical waves.

Gamma rays

X rays

Ultraviolet light

Metal fatigue t

X ray

Infrared waves

Sunbed

Visible light

Radar waves

Camera

UHF, VHF

ONE RANGE, MANY USE
Electric and magnetic waves are all part of one spectrum, or range. Their different wavelengths enable us to use them in many different ways.

Microwave oven

Radio waves

Radar

TV

Radio

Atoms and molecules

In the 1600s Irish-born Robert Boyle discovered that air is made up of tiny "corpuscles," or molecules. But what were they? In the 1770s French scientist Antoine Lavoisier found that when substances burn, they absorb something from the air. He named this "something" oxygen and realized it was an element—a pure ingredient that is able to combine with other elements in chemical reactions. In 1803 John Dalton of England saw that each element is made up of many identical particles—atoms—that can react with others to make molecules. In 1869 Russian Dmitri Mendeléev discovered that some elements react more easily than others.

WHAT'S IN AN ATOM?
In an atom the tiniest particle of matter, electrons (blue), whiz around a nucleus of neutrons (black) and protons (red).

Electron
Proton
Neutron
Electron path

Italy's Amadeo Avogadro found that there are 50 quadrillion atoms in less than one ounce of carbon.

PURE GENIUS
Einstein's equation $E = mc^2$ predicts the energy released by a split atom. The energy (E) equals the lost mass (m) times the speed of light (c) squared.

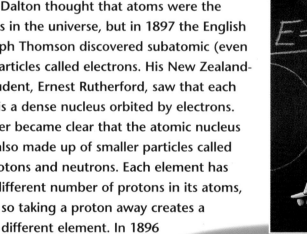

Subatomic

John Dalton thought that atoms were the smallest things in the universe, but in 1897 the English physicist Joseph Thomson discovered subatomic (even smaller) particles called electrons. His New Zealand-born student, Ernest Rutherford, saw that each atom is a dense nucleus orbited by electrons. It later became clear that the atomic nucleus is also made up of smaller particles called protons and neutrons. Each element has a different number of protons in its atoms, so taking a proton away creates a different element. In 1896 Frenchman Antoine-Henri Becquerel discovered the radioactive element uranium, which loses its protons naturally. In 1919 Rutherford managed to deliberately split an atom, releasing an enormous amount of energy compared with the size of the atom and giving us nuclear power.

Electrons are too small to see, but in 1911 Scotland's Charles Wilson invented the cloud chamber, a device to track their movements.

FUSION—THE FUTURE?
A fusion reaction occurs when atoms are joined. One day fusion reactors like this could give us clean, safe nuclear power.

FISSION BOMB
An atom can be split by firing another particle at it. The split pieces may hit other atoms; these also split. This is a fission reaction. A rapid chain of fission reactions releases enough energy to set off a nuclear explosion.

MARIE CURIE
This Polish-born physicist and her French husband, Pierre, studied radioactivity together. In 1898 they discovered the elements radium and polonium.

VITAL DISCOVERIES

For centuries people believed that Earth was only a few thousand years old and that all life was created in seven days. But many visionary scientists have changed that view forever.

Spinning Earth

Around A.D. 140 the astronomer Ptolemy declared that the Sun and the planets revolved around Earth. His system was accepted until 1543 when Poland's Nicolaus Copernicus suggested that Earth moves around the Sun. Italian Galileo Galilei proved him right in 1609 using the first real telescope. He concluded that Earth is a planet too. In the 1790s Scottish geologist James Hutton suggested that Earth was older than most people thought and had evolved over time. But it was over 100 years before another new science—nuclear physics—showed that our planet is over four billion years old.

ORRERY
This orrery, an 18th-century working model of our solar system, shows how the planets orbit the Sun.

Galileo's space discoveries upset leaders of the church. In 1632, under threat of torture, he had to "confess" that he was wrong.

DATABANK

Q When did life first appear on Earth, and what sort of life was it?

A The first life-forms were like bacteria, and they appeared around 3.8 billion years ago.

Q How long was it before the first animals developed, and where did they live?

A Complex sea animals probably appeared about three billion years later.

DINO CRISIS
In 1980 American Luis Alvarez suggested that dinosaurs were wiped out by an asteroid strike 65 million years ago.

World in action

In 1912 Alfred Wegener, a German weather expert, published a book showing that Africa and South America had once been joined together and that the continents had slowly drifted across the globe. Most geologists disputed his idea. Wegener had been dead 30 years by the time American geologist Harry Hess and others discovered that the Atlantic Ocean floor really is spreading. In the 1960s they showed that Earth's crust is divided into plates that can drift apart very slowly, crunch together, and grind past one another, causing earthquakes and volcanoes. This theory is called plate tectonics.

EARTH MOVER
The rock plates on which Africa and the Americas sit are slowly drifting apart. The plates "grow" outward from cracks in the mid-Atlantic seabed. Here they are "fed" by rising magma (very hot liquid rock) that hardens as it cools.

250 million years ago

100 million years ago

50 million years ago

Today

OUR CHANGING CONTINENTS
These globes show how landmasses have slowly drifted around the world, splitting, colliding, and sliding against one another.

HURRIED INTO PRINT
Darwin had to publish his theory of evolution in a rush in 1859; another scientist, Alfred Russel Wallace, had the same idea!

Infinite variety

Before Darwin, Frenchman Jean Lamarck thought animals passed on what they learned to their young.

In the 1700s Swedish scientist Carl Linnaeus invented a system of Latin names (still in use today) to show how different life-forms, or species, are related. Later scientists, studying old fossils, suspected that similar species might have come from the same ancestor, changing over time. But how? Englishman Charles Darwin explained it in 1859—random life-forms arise, and some are better equipped than others in the struggle for survival. Over time this leads to the evolution of new species.

LIFE HISTORY
The ancestors of fish, dinosaurs, humans, and all other life-forms originated in the ocean billions of years ago.

FACTS AND FIGURES

Scotsman James Hutton founded the basic principles of geology in the 1780s with "Theories of the Earth."

Some 19th-century scientists believed that God had put fossils in rocks deliberately to test their religious faith.

In 1907 New Zealander Ernest Rutherford used the natural radioactivity in rocks to measure their age.

In 1972 England's James Lovelock suggested that Earth has a survival instinct, an idea called the Gaia hypothesis.

In 1997 the Roslin Institute used sheep DNA to make a copy, or clone.

In 1953 American scientist Stanley Miller tried to create DNA by electrifying various gases. He succeeded only in making some proteins.

Genetic milestones

Darwin's theory depended on living things being different from their parents. In the 1850s an Austrian monk, Gregor Mendel, studied plants and saw that the differences are controlled by inherited particles called genes. In the early 1900s American zoologist Thomas Hunt Morgan found that genes are carried in parts of cells called chromosomes. Genes are a type of code written on a complex molecule—deoxyribonucleic acid, or DNA.

It was 1953 before American James Watson and Francis Crick of England, helped by the research of English scientist Rosalind Franklin, discovered how DNA worked. Human DNA carries about 30,000 genes in a chemical code of three billion units. In 1990 the Human Genome Project began work on identifying the entire code. It produced a first rough "gene map" in 2000.

DNA'S AMAZING VARIETY
We are all different because we inherit our own unique blend of genes from our parents. The chromosomes in our cells carry this gene "blueprint."

GENE TEAM
James Watson and Francis Crick won a Nobel Prize in 1962 for their work on DNA—the building block of life.

CRUCIAL INVENTIONS

While scientific study unravels the mysteries of nature, technology turns that knowledge into practical use. It helps us design and build machines that enable us to create civilizations.

WIND UP
One of the first known inventors was Archimedes. Around 250 B.C. this ancient Greek designed the Archimedes' screw, a tool for pumping water out of leaky ships. Its basic principle is still a feature of machines today.

Power and industry

For thousands of years human technology was limited by human strength. But at some point in prehistory people started inventing machines. One of the earliest was the lever, used to raise the colossal stones of Stonehenge in England. Then came the wheel, and by harnessing animals to wheeled vehicles people created the first bulk transportation system. Wheels also featured in water mills and windmills to turn the forces of nature into power. The inventors of these machines are unknown, but by the 1700s inventors, such as Thomas Newcomen and James Watt, had found ways of using steam power that helped create the modern industrial world.

WHEELS 'R' US
The wheel, in use by 3,500 B.C. in the Near East, has featured in almost every important mechanical tool or invention from ancient times to the present day.

REVOLUTIONARY WORKHORSE
The very efficient steam engines of Scotsman James Watt helped power British industry. This is a 1783 design.

Time and space

The ancient Egyptians measured time on sundials. Later they invented clocks controlled by dripping water. The first good mechanical clocks kept time using a pendulum, but the invention of the sprung balance wheel in the 1400s enabled people to carry pocket watches. Most modern wrist watches are electronic, controlled by the way a quartz crystal vibrates when electrified. Best of all are atomic clocks, which rely on the vibration of atoms millions of times per second.

Before they had effective clocks the Arabs perfected a device called the astrolabe, which used the sun and the stars to tell time.

MAKE IT A DATE
The Aztecs of South America used this stone calendar. At its center is the face of their sun god, Tonatiuh.

LCD WATCH
The numbers on the liquid crystal display (LCD) are lit by electrifying a special liquid behind a glass panel.

SWING IN TIME
The Dutch astronomer and physicist Christiaan Huygens built the first working pendulum clock in 1657.

CHRONOMETER
This clock, made by England's John Harrison in 1762, kept perfect time and helped sailors plot accurate routes.

THE WRITE STUFF
The ballpoint pen was invented as early as 1895, but Hungary's Laszlo Biro improved it in 1938—and gave it his name.

SWITCHED ON
The electric lightbulb was the invention of British Sir Joseph Swan and American Thomas Alva Edison in 1878–1879.

Top inventors

Some people have a talent for invention. The 16th-century Italian painter and scientist Leonardo da Vinci drew plans for many inventions, including a helicopter and a battle tank. Most were never built. The real age of invention arrived in the 1800s alongside electricity. In Great Britain, Michael Faraday invented the generator and the electric motor. In the U.S., Thomas Edison's many new ideas included the electric light, the first sound recorder, the telegraph, and the movie camera.

YOU CAN COUNT ON IT
The big, mechanical "difference engines" of Charles Babbage (1791–1871) were the first digital calculators—and the ancestors of today's computers.

Inventors protect their ideas from theft with a patent (ownership claim). Thomas Edison patented 1,093 inventions!

EASY DOES IT
The electric motor, first tested in 1821 by Michael Faraday, is used today in state-of-the-art machines like this computer-controlled robotic hand.

Thinking machines

It's hard to believe that 50 years ago computers barely existed! German Gottfried Leibniz came up with a simple calculating machine in 1671. By 1801 Frenchman Joseph-Marie Jacquard had a silk-weaving loom "programmed" by hole-punched cards, and in the 1830s England's Charles Babbage programmed mechanical calculators.

The integrated circuit was invented in 1958–1959 by Americans Jack Kilby and Robert Noyce, who worked separately on the idea.

The first real computers, such as ENIAC, an American design of 1945, were operated by bulky valves. Transistors replaced valves in 1948, and ten years later Intel's first silicon chip (also called an integrated circuit, or microchip) made personal computers a reality. Today a typical PC has more power than the computers that first sent men to the Moon.

FACTS AND FIGURES

The abacus, a counting system using rows of beads, was invented in China around 2,000 years ago.

Stonehenge, built in Bronze-Age England, may have worked as a calendar to track the sun and moon.

In 1876 Scotland's Alexander Graham Bell patented the telephone—just hours ahead of a rival phone inventor.

In the 1800s Lady Ada Lovelace, daughter of poet Lord Byron, was the first computer programmer.

In 1997 the IBM computer Deep Blue used its rapid calculating powers to beat the world chess champion, Garry Kasparov.

BYTE SIZE
Microchips are smaller than coins. Nanocomputers will one day have atom-sized components and astonishing power.

INSIDE A PC
A PC has memory and logic circuits. Data is loaded on to the hard drive from a floppy disk or CD. The screen image is controlled with the keyboard or mouse. PCs can now run Digital Versatile Disks, or DVDs—disks that carry video.

Screen

Logic circuits

Floppy disk

Compact disc

Keyboard

Hard drive

Mouse

MEDICAL BREAKTHROUGHS

The first true scientists were doctors—pioneers who rejected the magic and superstition of ancient medical practices and tried to understand exactly how the body worked in order to discover the real causes of disease.

REPAIR MAN
The Roman doctor Galen of Pergamum started his career healing gladiators wounded in the Roman arenas.

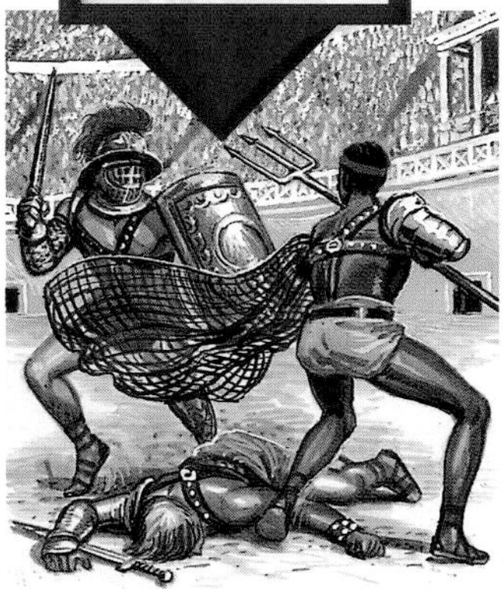

Foundations of medicine

In ancient Greece, Hippocrates based his ideas on observation as we do today—but he also believed that the balance of four "humors" (fluids) in the body was necessary for health. Roman doctor Galen took up this incorrect idea, and his books misled medicine until the 1500s when Swiss doctor Paracelsus rejected Galen's ideas. Instead Paracelsus worked on using chemicals as medicines. Meanwhile, in Belgium, André Vesalius was dissecting corpses to see how the body really worked. It was his findings, published in 1543, that launched modern medicine.

The ancient Greek medical pioneer Hippocrates cultivated more than 400 medicinal herbs in his physic garden.

STRANGE BREW
Ancient Egyptians knew a little about medicine, but they also tried to cure sick people with "magic" potions.

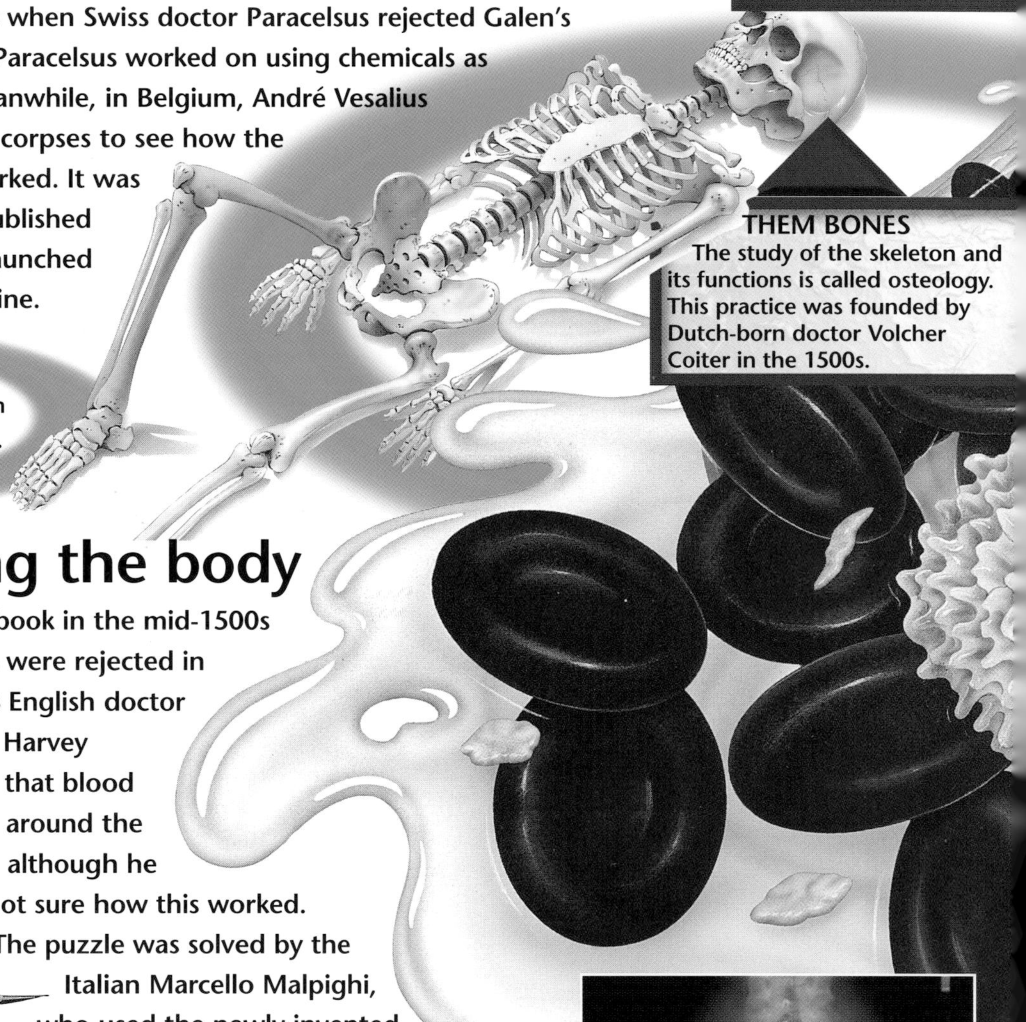

THEM BONES
The study of the skeleton and its functions is called osteology. This practice was founded by Dutch-born doctor Volcher Coiter in the 1500s.

Understanding the body

After Vesalius produced his anatomy book in the mid-1500s the mystical ideas of the Middle Ages were rejected in favor of a scientific approach. In 1628 English doctor William Harvey found that blood flows around the body, although he was not sure how this worked. The puzzle was solved by the Italian Marcello Malpighi, who used the newly invented microscope to reveal tiny blood vessels in the lungs. In Germany, Theodor Schwann used a microscope in the 1830s to find that the body is made of tiny cells. Twenty years later Rudolf Virchow worked out a whole system of disease and medicine based on the way cells work.

UP CLOSE
Dutch eyeglass maker Zacharias Janssen invented the microscope in 1590. In 1674 Antonie van Leeuwenhoek used this simple microscope to look at bacteria such as the *Salmonella* germ shown below.

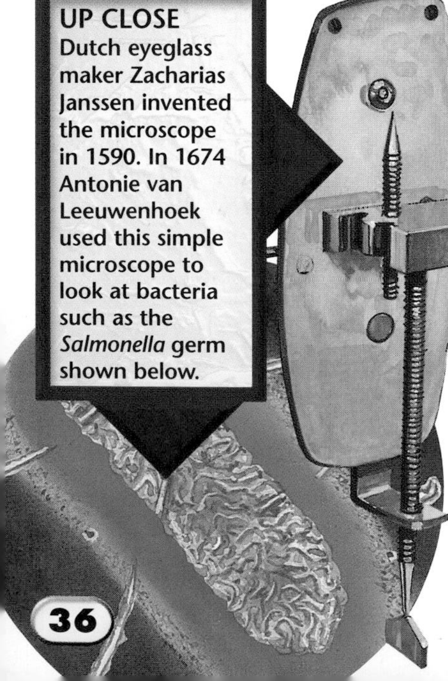

INSIDE VIEW
X rays, discovered by Germany's Wilhelm Röntgen in 1895, allowed doctors to look inside a patient's body without surgery.

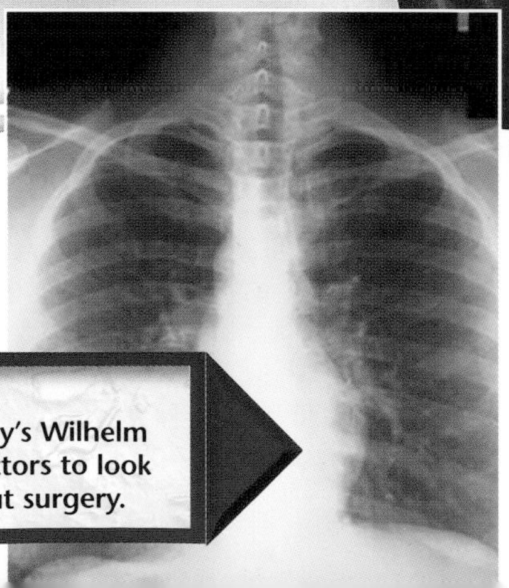

FACTS AND FIGURES

Acupuncture, a treatment involving needles stuck in the skin, was developed in China over 4,500 years ago.

The ideas of Roman doctors were copied into Arabic and used in the East. They were revived in medieval Europe.

In 1753 England's James Lind showed that scurvy, a disease that killed sailors, was caused by a lack of vitamin C.

Until the discovery of ether and chloroform in the 1840s surgery was performed without proper anesthesia.

Lifesavers

By the 1800s doctors knew the body fairly well, but infectious diseases were still a mystery. In 1796 Englishman Edward Jenner discovered vaccination and used it to prevent smallpox, but he did not know how it worked. Then in the 1860s Louis Pasteur of France showed that infections are caused by microorganisms, or germs. The idea inspired English surgeon Joseph Lister to use antiseptic sprays during operations. These were very successful in killing germs. In the 1870s Germany's Robert Koch discovered the bacterium that causes tuberculosis and founded the science of bacteriology. But the first effective antibacterial agent, penicillin, was not discovered until 1928—and it took until 1943 to develop it into an antibiotic drug.

LOUIS PASTEUR
His germ research led to the use of antiseptics—one of the greatest life-saving advances of the 1800s.

POX KILLER
A vaccine taken from victims of cowpox enabled Edward Jenner to protect people against smallpox, a terrible disease.

SPANISH INFLUENZA
In 1918–1919 this virus killed almost 22 million people worldwide. By 1933 scientists had discovered drugs that could control flu.

In 1850s France, Claude Bernard promoted chemical analysis as a medical tool—one that we take for granted today.

KILLER VIRUS
This human cell is infected with HIV, the human immunodeficiency virus, which causes the incurable AIDS disease.

DATABANK

STUFF OF LIFE
Blood is pumped around the body, carrying oxygen and nutrients to and from the organs. English scientist William Hewson (1739–1774) discovered the protein in our blood that helps it clot (turn thick and sticky).

Q What is the Hippocratic Oath?

A Named after a Greek doctor, it is a promise made by doctors to behave professionally.

Q When was the first successful human heart transplant, and who performed it?

A In 1967 South African Christiaan Barnard replaced the heart of Louis Washkansky.

Q Who invented the stethoscope?

A French doctor René Laënnec invented this simple listening instrument around 1816.

Q Who first discovered that infection with the HIV virus could develop into AIDS?

A The discovery by Luc Montagnier and Robert Gallo was announced in the U.S. in 1984.

ROAD AND RAIL

Two thousand years ago the Romans proved that a good road network is the backbone of civilization. Today there are few corners of the inhabited world without road or rail transportation.

FULL STEAM AHEAD
The world's first car was a steam-powered three-wheeler built by French engineer Nicholas-Joseph Cugnot in 1769.

Paving the way

The first true roads were built around the time wheeled vehicles came into use, some 5,000 years ago. The Minoans of Crete and the Egyptians built stone roads in the third millennium B.C., and the Assyrians used a 1,488-mi. (2,400-km) -long highway from the Mediterranean Sea to the Persian Gulf. The greatest road builders were the Romans. From 334 B.C. on they laid routes from their capital, Rome, across Italy and into France, Spain, Greece, and Africa. In all, 49,600 mi. (80,000km) of roads served their great empire. Chariots rattled along them, covering up to 75 mi. (120km) per day.

THE HARD WAY
All Roman roads were straight and very well drained. Most were made from rubble, sand, and large stones.

In 1934 Englishman Percy Shaw invented Cat's-eyes, the glass reflectors in the road that help drivers see at night or in fog.

FACTS AND FIGURES

- The Incas of South America sent all of their messages along the roads carried by foot couriers.

- On Nullarbor Plain, Australia, the Transcontinental Railway runs for a record 296 mi. in a completely straight line.

- Up to 12,000 workers died building the 47 mi. (76km) Panama Railroad in Central America in 1850–1858.

- Germany's Karl Benz created the first gasoline-driven car in 1886. It had three wheels and a top speed of 9mph.

- Protective airbags, designed at General Motors in 1973, became standard issue in 1988 on Chrysler cars.

OLD JAM
Carriages overload a street in London, England, in 1910. Today car traffic is a major problem. Critical Mass, a global cycling movement launched in 1992, campaigns in the streets for the use of bikes instead of cars.

The open road

The trusty Roman road design was not updated much until the late 1700s. Pierre Trésaguet in France and Thomas Telford in Scotland both invented new, lightweight road surfaces. In the 1790s John McAdam, another Scotsman, invented the tough "macadam" surface of crushed stones. By the 1880s people wanted a smooth ride for their bicycles, which were becoming popular, so a Belgian named Edward De Smedt tested an asphalt surface in New York and Washington, D.C. Asphalt is still in use today.

With the rise of car use in the 1900s road construction boomed. The first full highway network was developed in Adolf Hitler's Nazi Germany in 1935–1942. Today the United States has four million mi. (6.4 million km) of roads—more than any other country.

DEAD END?
Today many people oppose new road projects because of damage caused to the environment. They would rather see money spent on public transportation.

The rearview mirror was invented in 1897 by Frenchwoman Davy de Cussé. A reporter said, "It's a weird contraption that has no future."

MODEL EMPLOYER
When Henry Ford, founder of Ford cars, slashed the price of his Model T and paid his workers higher wages, sales soared!

FASTEST PORSCHE OF ITS DAY
The Porsche 959, built in 1987–1988, has a 0–60mph time of 3.7 seconds and a top speed of more than 190 mph.

The car

The first gasoline cars of the 1880s were handmade luxuries that only a few families could afford. But mass production, introduced by the companies Oldsmobile and Ford in the early 1900s, led to cheaper cars. Ford sold more than 15 million Model Ts, and the U.S. led the world in car production until Japan took over in the 1980s. Today's most popular cars are small and economical to run, and some can be recycled. Carmakers are also testing "clean" fuels such as natural gas and hydrogen. But luxury cars, such as Ferrari and Rolls Royce, still survive.

In 1890 William Morrison of Iowa invented an electric car that could run for 13 hours at 14 mph (22km/h).

WIZARD OF OZ
Sunraycer won the 1987 World Solar Challenge in Australia. Built by General Motors, it had an electric motor powered by 5 kWh of solar cells. Covering 1,867 mi., it went an average speed of 42 mph.

Station to station

In Great Britain the railroad was developed as a faster alternative to transporting goods by canal, but engineers soon spotted its potential for transporting passengers. In 1825–1830 George Stephenson designed the first railroads and their trains in northern England. Rail networks soon covered Europe and the U.S., where the line to the Pacific opened by 1869. By 1917 there were more than one million mi. (1.5 million km) of tracks in the world. Diesel- and electric-powered trains took over from steam in the 1930s, though Africa, India, and China still run steam trains. Today people want to travel fast—France's TGV train can make the 682 mi. (1,100km) run from Calais to Marseille in 3 hours, 29 minutes at an average speed of 342 mph (306km/h).

GOING LOCO
George Stephenson's *Rocket* won the 1829 Rainhill trials, reaching 36 mph. It ran on England's Liverpool and Manchester Railway, opened in 1830.

India has the largest railroad network in Asia, carrying over 11 million passengers each day and 380 million tons of freight each year.

THE FUTURE OF RAILROADS?
Maglev trains use electromagnets to float at very high speed along special tracks. In 1999 a Japanese maglev reached 342 mph.

SEA AND AIR

Water transport used to be the quickest form of transportation. Today air travel has taken the lead and is getting faster all of the time.

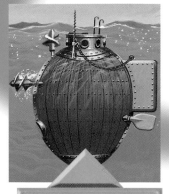

ONE-MAN MENACE
The 1775 *Turtle* was the first military submarine, built by American David Bushnell to plant mines on British ships.

Know your knots

The first "boats" were probably logs used as rafts to cross rivers. Other early boats were made from clay pots or animal hides and were paddled by hand or by oar. Then people found that the wind could be harnessed for power. The Egyptians used a simple square sail, but from the 100s A.D. this gave way to the triangular lateen sail, originally an Arab design. Wooden sailing ships ruled the seas until the 1800s. The most graceful were the long, slender tea clippers, first built in the United States in the 1800s. Steamships eventually took over from sailing ships, since they worked when there was no wind. Most ships today are driven by oil, although many submarines and warships rely on nuclear power.

Iron-hulled ships were introduced in the 1800s to withstand damage from exploding shells, which could rip wooden ships apart.

AMERICAN BEAUTIES
Tea clippers, the fastest commercial ships of their day, were designed to rush the tea crop from China to the United States.

Sea powers

From around 1000 B.C. to A.D. 1000 the Phoenicians, the Greeks, the Romans, and the Byzantines ruled Mediterranean waters with fleets of oared galleys. With the decline of Rome the Mediterranean Sea and Indian Ocean were dominated by Muslim fleets and later by the Turkish Ottoman empire. The Ottoman fleet was defeated in 1571 by Spain and Venice at the Battle of Lepanto near Greece. After crushing the Spanish Armada in 1588 England—later Great Britain and its Royal Navy—became a major sea power. During World War II the United States defeated Japan's Imperial Navy in battles between aircraft carriers in the Pacific, and in the Atlantic the Allies finally defeated Nazi Germany's U-boats.

IRONCLAD
Built by England's Isambard Kingdom Brunel, the *Great Eastern* was the largest vessel of its day in 1858. A cable-laying ship, it used sails, paddle engines, or propeller engines depending on the conditions.

BOMBS AWAY!
Today the greatest naval fleets are the U.S. Sixth and Seventh Fleets. Here a fighter bomber prepares for take-off from a carrier.

History of flight

The first successful manned flights were in balloons designed by France's Montgolfier brothers in the late 1700s. Englishman George Cayley tested the first manned glider in 1853, inspiring German Otto Lilienthal and French-born Octave Chanute to produce their own glider designs. In 1903 the Wright brothers made the first powered flight.

UP, UP, AND AWAY
In 1783 the Marquis d'Arlandes and Pilâtre de Rozier drifted over Paris in a Montgolfier hot-air balloon.

THE WRIGHT STUFF
In 1903 Orville (right) and Wilbur Wright made the first powered, controlled, and sustained flight in *Flyer I* near Kitty Hawk, North Carolina.

Flight development gathered speed in the world wars of 1914–1918 and 1939–1945 as the opposing sides fought for control of the skies. Late in World War II, Germany's Messerschmitt Me 262 became the first jet to fly in combat. It had a top speed of almost 550 mph (885km/h). The jet engine was based on a design by British engineer Frank Whittle. Also of British design was the De Havilland Comet, the first large commercial jet airplane, first used in 1952. Jet airplanes are now the main form of air travel.

FACTS AND FIGURES

The Italian genius and painter Leonardo da Vinci made drawings of helicopters and flying machines in 1483.

Paul Cornu, a French engineer, made the first flight in a helicopter in 1907. It flew for around 20 seconds.

With a 246 ft. wingspan, the solar-powered Helios "flying wing" reaches altitudes of up to 98,200 ft.

Currently being built by Airbus, the A380 superjumbo is an airplane that will carry over 650 passengers.

Flight deck

First-class cabin

Crew rest

Economy seats

JUMBO JET
The Boeing 747 was first used in 1970 and is still in use today. The 747-400 can carry up to 524 passengers.

Forward cargo

Wing gear

Rolls-Royce engine

New and unusual aircraft

In 1968 the Soviet Union flew the world's first supersonic (faster than sound) transport (SST), the Tupolev Tu-144. Concorde, an SST built by Great Britain and France, made its first test flight in 1969. Concordes still fly, despite a serious crash in July 2000. Future passenger SSTs may fly faster than today's planes by briefly escaping Earth's atmosphere to travel in near-space conditions.

Military craft include many unusual designs. The U.S. stealth bomber is designed so that it cannot be traced by enemy radar. Begun in secret in 1982, it was unveiled in 1988.

HIDDEN JET
The peculiar shape and special wing coating of the American B-2 stealth bomber make it invisible to enemy radar.

RESEARCH ON THE WING
A drone (pilotless plane) is launched from a huge B-52 bomber to perform tests for NASA.

BUILDINGS AND MONUMENTS

Whether built for offering devotion to a god or for housing a ruler, great buildings and monuments show what can be achieved when people work together.

Ancient sites

Ancient builders had no machinery so the work that went into projects such as the Egyptian pyramids—colossal tombs for the pharaohs—can only be marveled at. The Great Pyramid in Giza is 458 ft. (140m) high. Native peoples in North and South America built pyramids to be used as temples. As early as 12,000 B.C. people in Europe built stone circles. Small circles were used as animal pens. Large circles, such as Stonehenge and Avebury in England, were probably used in religious rituals.

PETRA: CITY IN STONE
Petra (in modern-day Jordan) was begun in the 400s B.C. by the Nabatean Arabs. Its rose-red buildings are carved into the walls of a sandstone valley.

POINTS MADE
The pyramids of Egypt were built 4,500 years ago from millions of stone blocks that weigh an average 2.3 tons each.

IN THE RING
The Colosseum was a giant, free-standing stadium in ancient Rome. Constructed from concrete and stone around A.D. 80, it could seat 50,000 spectators and was the scene of savage fights between animals and gladiators.

The Temple of Artemis at Ephesus (modern-day Turkey) was a huge Greek temple with 106 columns, each 39 ft. (12m) high.

Places of worship

Many of the world's finest buildings have a religious use. The Great Mosque in Mecca, in modern-day Saudi Arabia, encloses the Kaaba, a cubic building, which Muslims believe is the world's first building of worship. Angkor Wat in Cambodia was built in the 1100s to honor the Hindu god Vishnu. Shaped like a pyramid, it covers almost one square mile (2.6 km²). In Java, Indonesia, is the Buddhist temple of Borobudur. Built in the 700s and 800s A.D., Borobudur was erected as a huge, square shell around a hill. Impressive Christian churches include Germany's Cologne Cathedral. The largest Gothic-style church in Europe, with two 514-ft. (157-m) -high towers, it took over 600 years to build! Begun in 1248, it was completed in 1880.

MUSLIM MASTERPIECE
The Blue Mosque in Istanbul, Turkey, is a Muslim center of worship. Built in 1609–1616, it has six minarets (towers) instead of four, which is more common.

One of India's greatest Hindu temples is at Srirangam in Tamil Nadu. It has an outer perimeter of around 2 mi. (3km).

BUDDHISM IN TIBET
In Lhasa, Tibet's capital, is the Buddhist temple of Gtsug-lag-khang. Built in the 600s A.D., it is Tibet's holiest site.

Architects

Behind every great building is an architect with a unique vision. In 16th-century Turkey, for example, Mimar Sinan designed the Mosque of Suleyman in Istanbul. In Chicago in the late 1800s Louis Sullivan designed the first skyscrapers. His assistant, Frank Lloyd Wright, later eclipsed Sullivan's fame with his own elegant, rambling "Prairie-style" homes. Another giant of architecture is Antoni Gaudí of Spain. His Sagrada Familia, a pinnacled cathedral in Barcelona, was begun in 1882 but was still unfinished in 2003.

Le Corbusier of Switzerland was one of the most inventive architects of the 1900s. He once said, "A house is a machine for living in."

GLORIOUS DOME
Sir Christopher Wren (1632–1723) designed more than 50 London churches, including St. Paul's Cathedral (1710).

SPACE-AGE ART HOUSE
The Guggenheim Art Museum, built in Bilbao, Spain, in 1997, was designed by American Frank Gehry. It has glass walls and a thin "skin" of titanium.

Monuments

Monuments are usually built in memory of an event, a place, or a person, but Egypt's Great Sphinx—a huge stone lion with a human head—is a mystery. It may have been built as a guardian. The Colossos of Rhodes was another guardian, a 27-ft. (37-m) -high bronze statue that stood at the mouth of Rhodes harbor by the Aegean Sea until it was toppled by an earthquake in 224 B.C. The Buddha of Leshan, China, built in A.D. 713–803, is 236 ft. (72m) high and is the world's tallest Buddha. In St. Louis, Missouri, the 629-ft. (192-m) -high Gateway Arch was erected in 1965 to honor American settlers of the 1800s.

FACTS AND FIGURES

The Wailing Wall, sacred to Jews, is the last remains of a temple in Jerusalem ransacked by the Romans around A.D. 70.

The amazing shell-shaped Sydney Opera House in Australia was the vision of Danish architect Jørn Utzon.

Architects Oscar Niemeyer and Lúcio Costa built the center of Brasilia, the capital city of their native Brazil, in 1960.

The world's largest Christian church is the basilica of Our Lady of Peace in Côte d'Ivoire, West Africa. It seats 18,000!

TORCHBEARER
One of New York's best-loved landmarks is the 301-ft. (92-m) -tall Statue of Liberty, set up in 1886 to celebrate the friendship between the U.S. and France. She holds a torch and a tablet inscribed with the date July 4, 1776.

TAJ MAHAL
This huge marble tomb in India was built by Shah Jahan in 1632–1649 in memory of his favorite wife, Mumtaz Mahal.

MIGHTY STRUCTURES

Since ancient times engineers have pushed the limits of achievement. From tunnels to skyscrapers, big projects demonstrate human skill and inspiration on a truly grand scale.

Reach for the sky

One of the first skyscrapers was the The Wainwright Building in St. Louis, Missouri (1891). In New York City in 1930 the Empire State Building (1,247 ft./381m) and the Chrysler Building (1,044 ft./319m) went up. The World Trade Center's twin towers won at 1,365 ft. (417m) in 1973. Sadly, on September 11, 2001 they were destroyed in a terrorist attack. Chicago's Sears Tower (1,450 ft./443m) was built in 1974. Today's tallest buildings are Malaysia's Petronas Towers (1,479 ft.), but Toronto's CN TV mast is 1,810 ft. tall.

The next "world's tallest skyscraper" is likely to be the Shanghai World Financial Center in China, which aims to break 1,640 ft. (500m).

ROOM TO GROW
Home to space shuttles, the Vehicle Assembly Building in Florida has a vast volume of 13.06 million ft³.

THE LONG HAUL
The steel beams that support a skyscraper appear I-shaped from the end—this strong design resists bending and buckling.

Great bridges

Bridge building symbolizes humankind's ability to overcome obstacles—and New York's Brooklyn Bridge is no exception. Construction, begun in 1869, was completed in 1883—despite an explosion, a fire, faulty cables, and the death of its planner, John Roebling. It once had the longest main span of any bridge in the world. Today the world's longest bridge is the Pontchartrain Causeway in Louisiana, which crosses 24 mi. (38.4km) of water. One of the longest suspension bridges is California's Golden Gate Bridge, but with a main span of 6,518 ft. (1,991m), the Akashi-Kaikyo bridge is the longest.

SUPER SPAN
Completed in 1937, the Golden Gate Bridge links California with the San Francisco peninsula. The main span of the bridge's roadway is 4,190 ft. long. It is suspended on 236-in.-thick steel cables hung from two 743 ft. towers.

SPACE NEEDLE
Opened for the 1962 World's Fair, the 607-ft.-high Space Needle gives visitors a panoramic view of Seattle, Washington. From its top a beam of light, the Legacy Light, is shined skyward on special occasions.

Dams

The world's tallest dam is the Rogun on the Vakhsh River in Tajikistan. Completed in 1987, it is 1,097 ft. (335m) high. The largest dam by volume of water is the Syncrude Tailings Dam in Canada, which holds back 1.8 billion ft.³ (540 million m³) of water.

HYDROELECTRIC POWER
Dams are constructed across deep river valleys. The dammed water rushes down through turbines to generate electricity.

The ancient Vietnamese citadel of Hué is circled by an 6.8-mi.-long wall. It took 20,000 workers to build the 33-ft.-thick defenses.

Walls

Probably the greatest-ever building project is the Great Wall of China. Most of the 3,968-mi. (6,400-km) -long wall dates from the time of the Ming dynasty (1368–1644). It was probably built to show off the power of the emperors and was used as a line of defense against warlike tribes. A smaller defensive wall, 73 mi. (117km) long, was built in Great Britain by the Roman emperor Hadrian in A.D. 126.

WRATH OF KHAN
China's Great Wall was no defense against Genghis Khan, whose Mongol warriors burst through it in 1215.

WORK TO RULE
The foreman in charge of construction makes sure that his builders follow the instructions of the architect.

Tunnels

Japan is the home of the world's longest tunnel, the Seikan rail tunnel, which is 33 mi. (53.9km) long and was opened in 1988. It connects the main Japanese island of Honshu with its northern neighbor, Hokkaido. Slightly shorter is the Channel Tunnel between Great Britain and France. Completed in 1994, it is just under 30 mi. (50km) long.

USING A TUNNEL-BORER
Bits in the front of this machine are pushed forward to smash the rock. The debris is removed and then a concrete safety lining is sprayed on the newly dug walls.

FACTS AND FIGURES

Opened in 1914, the Panama Canal shortened a ship's route from New York City to San Francisco by 8,990 mi.

The largest single-unit radio telescope at the Arecibo Observatory in Puerto Rico measures 998 ft. in diameter.

The 363-ft.-high Aswan Dam, completed in 1970, controls the floodwaters of the Nile River in Egypt.

There are plans to build a 2,183-ft.-high tower in Katangi, India, but it will not be ready before 2008.

The 40 mi. (65km) Panama Canal took ten years to build. The workers had to cut through jungles infested with malarial mosquitoes.

Canals

At 1,083 mi. (1,747km), the world's longest artificial waterway is the Chinese Grand Canal. The oldest section of the canal, begun in 486 B.C., was rebuilt in A.D. 607 and is still in use today. In 1859–1869 Frenchman Ferdinand de Lesseps built the 103 mi. (166km) Suez Canal across Egypt to connect the Red Sea to the Mediterranean. A century later, in North America, the St. Lawrence Seaway linked the Great Lakes to the Atlantic Ocean.

FROM RED SEA TO MED SEA
Ships steam down the Suez Canal in 1869. Every day an average of 55 vessels use this waterway beween Africa and Asia.

THE OLYMPICS

In the Olympic Games, held every four years, the world's top athletes represent their countries and compete for medals. Gold, silver, and bronze are awarded for first, second, and third place.

The ancient games

The first recorded Olympics, in the Greek city of Olympia in 776 B.C., formed part of a ceremony honoring the god Zeus. The events included running, horse and chariot racing, discus, javelin, boxing, and wrestling. At first only Greek men took part. After the Romans conquered Greece events were open to men from all over the empire. A separate event, honoring the goddess Hera, is thought to have taken place for unmarried women.

WINNER TAKES ALL
In the Greek games a winner received a laurel wreath to wear. His home city also presented him with gifts and money.

Even in ancient Greece, Olympic athletes would hire coaches and eat special diets in an attempt to beat the competition.

POLITICS
Berlin, Germany, hosted the 1936 Olympics. With Nazi Adolph Hitler in power, the event was tense. In Los Angeles in 1984 the Soviet Union and other Communist teams stayed away due to bad relations with the U.S.

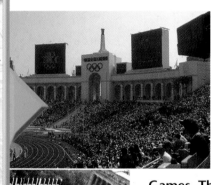

Olympic revival

The original Olympics ran every four years for 12 centuries until the Romans banned them in A.D. 393.

Frenchman Baron Pierre de Coubertin founded the modern Olympic Games. The first took place in Athens in 1896, with more than 280 athletes attending from 13 nations. Since then the Games have grown to include more nations and more sports—from sprinting to soccer and swimming to cycling. Gold medals were first awarded at the London Games in 1908. Women first competed—unofficially—in Paris in 1900, but they were restricted at first to golf and tennis. In 1928 women were officially included. In the 2000 Olympics, held in Sydney, Australia, 11,000 athletes from 200 nations participated.

HIGH FIVE
The five colored, linked rings, symbolizing the five inhabited continents, were first used in 1920.

DATABANK

Q Who has organized the Olympics ever since the 1896 Games?
A The International Olympic Committee (IOC) is in charge.

Q Why were the 1908 Games held in London, not in Rome as planned?
A The eruption of Mount Vesuvius in 1906 left Italy in turmoil.

Q Who is seen as the world's greatest hockey player?
A In his 20-year career Canada's Wayne Gretzky scored 1,072 goals.

Q Who is the world's fastest woman in the 100m sprint?
A Florence Griffith Joyner (U.S.) ran it in 10.49 seconds in 1988.

SNOW BUSINESS
Skiing first became an Olympic event in 1924. Events today include jumping, cross-country, slalom (weaving around flags), and downhill racing.

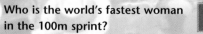

Great Olympians

American swimmer Mark Spitz won nine gold medals in 1968–1972, eight of them in record times. Hungarian fencer Aladár Gerevich won six golds in a row in 1932–1960, and British rower Steven Redgrave won five gold medals in 1984–2000. Dutchwoman Fanny Blankers-Koen won four track-and-field gold medals at the 1948 London Olympics. The greatest male long-distance runner is the Czech Emil Zatopek, who won 38 10,000-m races in a row between 1948 and 1956.

MARATHON
This 26-mi. race was first run in 490 B.C. by a Greek messenger after a battle victory at Marathon against the Persians.

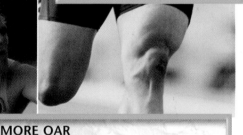

MIND, BODY, SPIRIT
Paralympics, Olympic games for the disabled, have been running since 1960. Here a competitor in a wheelchair race pushes toward the finish line.

WORLD'S FASTEST MAN
U.S. athlete Maurice Greene ran the 100-m sprint in a record 9.79 seconds in Athens in 1999 and then went on to win the gold medal at the 2000 Olympics.

MORE OAR
British rowers Steven Redgrave (left) and Matt Pinsent compete as a pair. Rowers also race in four- and eight-person crews.

FACTS AND FIGURES

U.S. athletes Jesse Owens (1936) and Carl Lewis (1984) have each won four golds in track-and-field events.

Finnish ski jumper Matt Nykanen has won a record four Olympic titles.

George Eyser (U.S.) won six gymnastics medals at the 1904 Olympics in St. Louis, despite having a wooden leg.

Germany's Katerina Witt won the Olympic and World Figure Skating Championships in both 1984 and 1988.

The first Special Olympics, games for athletes with learning difficulties, were held in 1968 in the United States.

Equestrianism (horse riding) is the only Olympic sport in which men and women compete as equals.

Olympics on ice

The Winter Olympics includes sports such as hockey, skiing, ice-skating, and bobsledding. They were first held in Chamonix, France, in 1924. The most successful countries, such as Norway, Austria, Switzerland, Russia, Germany, Canada, and Italy, have a tradition of winter sports, mostly because of their cold climate. Hockey is the main team sport of the event, and the United States, Canada, and Russia usually have strong teams. However both Canada and the United States lost to the Czech Republic in Nagano, Japan, in 1998.

Impressively, tropical Jamaica sent a bobsled team to the 1988 Olympics—and finished 14th, ahead of the U.S. sleds!

FLAT OUT
Luge is a winter Olympic sport. Competitors lie back on a sled to reduce drag, reaching speeds of 62 mph.

ON THE TEAM

A sports team can only be successful if all of its members work together. This is especially true in ball games, where everyone has an important part to play.

The world game

Soccer truly is a global sport. Over 150 countries try to reach the World Cup finals, which are held every four years. Brazil, with five World Cup wins, is regarded as the greatest soccer nation, followed by Germany and Italy, each with three wins. Europe has the largest number of professional soccer teams of any continent. The top prize in European championship soccer is the European Champion's Cup, or Champion's League. Spain's Real Madrid has won this cup eight times. Italy's AC Milan has five wins, and Germany's Bayern Munich, the Netherlands' Ajax, and England's Liverpool each have four.

WORLD CUP GIANTS
Brazil's soccer team has won the World Cup a record five times, winning in 1958, 1962, 1970, 1994 (below), and 2002.

In 1999 Manchester United topped England's Premier League and won both the Football Association Cup and the European Cup.

Run with it!

Rugby has two types: Union and League. Australia has won two of the four Union World Cups ever played and the eight League World Cups. Other Union giants are New Zealand's All Blacks and South Africa's Springboks. Australia's David Campese scored a record 64 tries in 101 games between 1982 and 1996. In 2001 Neil Jenkins of Wales became the first player to have scored 1,000 points.

In football U.S. teams play for the Super Bowl each year. The San Francisco 49ers and the Dallas Cowboys have each won it five times. With a record 420 touchdown passes, quarterback Dan Marino is one of football's all-time greats.

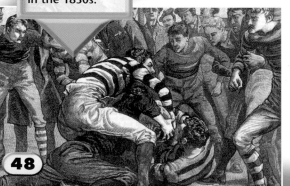

SCRUMMAGE
Rugby, a rough sport in which an oval ball is carried and kicked, was first played in England In the 1830s.

HOOLIGANS!
In medieval times soccer had no teams and few rules. Boys simply ran through the streets chasing a ball made from a pig's bladder. By 1314 England's King Edward II had banned the violent sport from London's streets.

FACTS AND FIGURES

Ferenc Puskas scored 83 goals in 84 games for Hungary—a record in international soccer.

The top scorer in National Basketball Association history is American Kareem Abdul-Jabbar, with 38,387 points.

The highest team score in international cricket is 952 for 6 declared by Sri Lanka against India in 1997.

In international soccer history Claudio Suárez of Mexico has clocked the most appearances as captain—165.

Between 1928 and 1968 Pakistan and India won every Olympic field hockey tournament between them.

PLAYING HARDBALL
Football players wear body padding. In this 1996 game Fred Strickland (55) of the Dallas Cowboys chases Terry Allen (21) of the Washington Redskins.

DATABANK

Q Who do most people consider to be the greatest soccer players of all time?

A Pele (Brazil), Diego Maradona (Argentina), and Ferenc Puskas (Hungary).

Q Which one-time medical student became known as the "Father of Football"?

A In 1880 Walter Chauncey Camp wrote most of the rules for this sport.

Mark McGwire of the St. Louis Cardinals baseball team hit a record 70 home runs in a single season (1998).

Bat and ball

Baseball is played mainly in North America and Cuba. The New York Yankees have won the World Series 26 times. Their best player ever, George Herman "Babe" Ruth, hit 714 home runs in his 1914–1938 career—a record beaten only by Hank Aaron with 755 home runs.

The first recorded cricket match took place in Kent, England, in 1646. Australia has produced the greatest team, winning 16 test matches in a row in 1999–2001. Top Australian batsman Don Bradman averaged 99 runs per innings. Brian Lara of the West Indies holds the highest individual score, 375, made against England in 1994.

WHATEVER THE WEATHER
The roof of the SkyDome stadium in Toronto, Canada, can be closed to keep the rain out. Built in 1989, SkyDome is the home of the Blue Jays baseball team.

MICHAEL JORDAN
Jordan led the Chicago Bulls to five NBA wins in 1991–1997, and his career average of 31.5 points per game is unequaled.

Basketball

Invented by James Naismith in 1981 as a game to stay in shape, basketball is now one of the United States' most popular sports. The NBA (National Basketball Association) championship has been won 16 times by the Boston Celtics. One of basketball's most popular players, Earvin "Magic" Johnson, led the L.A. Lakers to five NBA championships in 1980–1988. He was diagnosed HIV-positive in 1991 but returned as coach and later as a player.

Wilt Chamberlain scored 31,419 points in professional basketball during 1958–1973. "Wilt the Stilt" was over 6.9 ft. tall.

Women on the team

Until recently women's team sports did not receive as much recognition and support as men's teams. Today there are women's World Cups in soccer, cricket, rugby, field hockey, and skiing. The Women's Cricket World Cup has been held since 1973, and the 2000 champions were New Zealand. The United States has the most successful international women's soccer team. World champions in 1991 and 1999, they outshone the U.S. men's team.

STICKS UP
In field hockey women have played in the World Cup since 1975 and the Olympics since 1980. The most successful World Cup teams are the Netherlands, Germany, Argentina, and Australia.

SPORTS LEGENDS

Relying on their own fitness, skills, and temperament, some athletes rise above the competition to achieve true greatness and become legends.

First past the post

Achieving an important "first" wins a place in sports history. British runner Roger Bannister is still celebrated for being the first to run 1 mi. (1.6km) in under four minutes, a feat he performed in 1954. Maureen Connolly won the women's Wimbledon singles title in her first attempt in 1952. In 1975 Arthur Ashe became the first black winner at Wimbledon. That same year he won the World Championship singles.

In 1990 Pete Sampras, aged 19, became the youngest winner of tennis's U.S. Open. By 2001 he had won 13 Grand Slams.

LEAP OF GENIUS
Top show jumper Hugo Simon of Austria has won the World Cup three times: in 1979, 1996, and 1997.

BREAKING THE BARRIER
The first athlete to run the 100m sprint in 10 seconds was American Bob Hayes (second left) at the 1964 Tokyo Olympics.

FACTS AND FIGURES

In 1987 German Boris Becker, only 17, became the first unseeded (unranked) tennis player to win Wimbledon.

English riding jockey Lester Piggott had won 4,350 races when he left the saddle to become a trainer in 1985.

In 1999 Stephen Hendry of Scotland won his seventh world snooker title— a record total.

Speed kings

Formula One is the best-known championship in car racing. Argentina's Juan-Manuel Fangio won it five times during 1951–1957, though this record was later matched by Germany's Michael Schumacher, who won his fifth title in 2002. The year before Schumacher had scored his 52nd Grand Prix win, beating the previous record holder, Frenchman Alain Prost.

The greatest speed king on two wheels is Italy's Giacomo Agostini, who won 15 motorcycle world titles in his career, including eight at the prestigious 500cc level (equivalent to Formula One). Australia's Michael Doohan won five world titles in the 1990s.

The Indianapolis 500, an American race of 500 mi. (800km), has been won four times each by Al Unser, Rick Mears, and A. J. Foyt. Jr.

AND THEY'RE OFF!
Built in 1906, the 2.8 mi. Brooklands circuit in Surrey, England, was the world's first racing speedway.

BROOKLANDS

Simply the best

LEADER OF THE PACK
During each stage of the Tour de France, a bicycle race over 2,480 mi. (4,000km), the leader wears a special yellow shirt.

Every sport has its all-time legends. One such legend is American golfer Jack Nicklaus, who has won 18 Major golf tournaments between 1962 and 1986. Another American, Tiger Woods, winner of six Majors by 2001, could still beat Nicklaus. One of the most successful sportswomen ever is Czech-born Martina Navratilova, who won 168 single and 165 double tennis titles, including 56 Grand Slam victories. Pakistan's Jahangir Khan first won the World Open squash championship in 1981 at the age of 17. He went on to win the World Open ten times and the British Open ten times in a row and was undefeated for a record five-and-a-half years. One of the most famous sports figures of the last 100 years—calling himself "the greatest"— is American boxer Muhammad Ali. He won three world heavyweight titles during his career and has become a worldwide celebrity.

WHAT A RACKET
American Martina Navratilova was born in Czechoslovakia in 1956. Her tennis achievements include nine Wimbledon wins between 1978 and 1990.

Boxing gloves are believed to have been developed in ancient Crete. They can be seen in a painting from 1500 B.C.

In 1938 boxer Henry Armstrong held a record three world titles at once: feather, light, and welterweight.

SWING KING
Jack Nicklaus's career wins include three individual World Cups, four U.S. Opens, three British Opens, six Australian Opens, and six Masters. The tall, blond Nicklaus been nicknamed the "Golden Bear."

NUMBER ONE
Born in 1969, German Michael Schumacher began racing go-carts at the age of four. He won his first Formula One (F1) championship in 1994 behind the wheel of a Benetton-Ford. In 1996 Schumacher started driving for Team Ferrari. This is the car he used in the F1 world championship in 2002.

DATABANK

Q What is meant by a "Major" in golf or a "Grand Slam" in tennis?

A Majors are the top-four events in golf, and Grand Slams are the top-four events in tennis.

Q Who is the greatest female squash player of all time?

A Australian Heather Blundell lost only two squash matches in her 1959–1980 career.

Q Has anyone won both the motorcycle and Formula One racing world championships?

A Great Britain's John Surtees is the only winner of both two- and four-wheeled world championships.

EARLY PIONEERS

For early peoples the world stretched only as far as the hills or deserts on their horizon. But the efforts of explorers meant that more of the world was put on the map.

First treks

The first great seafarers of the Near East were the Phoenicians, who settled on the eastern Mediterranean coast. They sailed along North Africa, building trading cities such as Carthage in Tunisia (now Tunis). Around 600 B.C. the Egyptian king Necho hired Phoenician mariners to sail around Africa from the Arabian Gulf and through the Mediterranean. Three centuries later Alexander the Great of Macedonia (then a part of northern Greece) led war treks into Asia that were also voyages of discovery. He defeated the Persians and then marched on to India, taking Greek culture deep into Asia.

PACIFIC RACES
Waves of people, originally from Asia, moved east across the Pacific Ocean, settling on the thousands of islands that make up Oceania. The Polynesians (pictured) first settled on the Polynesian Islands 6,000 years ago.

North America

Central America   Car

NORSEMEN
Vikings explored the Atlantic more than 1,000 years ago. They found North America but did not settle there permanently.

In 500 B.C. Hanno of Carthage took 60 ships out of the Mediterranean and around West Africa to discover cities.

Age of Discovery

The 1400s heralded the Age of Discovery, when Europeans set out to trade and to found colonies. In 1492 Christopher Columbus, an Italian being paid by Spain, sailed west in search of a route to China but landed in North America—the first European to do so. From Spain came Vasco de Balboa, who crossed Panama to the American Pacific coast in 1513, and Hernan Cortes, who conquered Mexico in 1519. The same year Portugal's Ferdinand Magellan passed the tip of South America and set out across the Pacific. He was killed in the Philippines, but his crew returned safely, completing the first-ever around-the-world voyage.

By a 1494 treaty Portugal and Spain divided new lands. Spain took most of the Americas; Portugal took Brazil, plus lands to the east.

NEW GOODS
Spanish explorers brought potatoes, peppers, tomatoes, sunflowers, cocoa, pineapples, and tobacco back from North America.

MILES OUT
Columbus reached the Bahamas in 1492. He later visited Cuba, believing it to be Japan or the Chinese mainland.

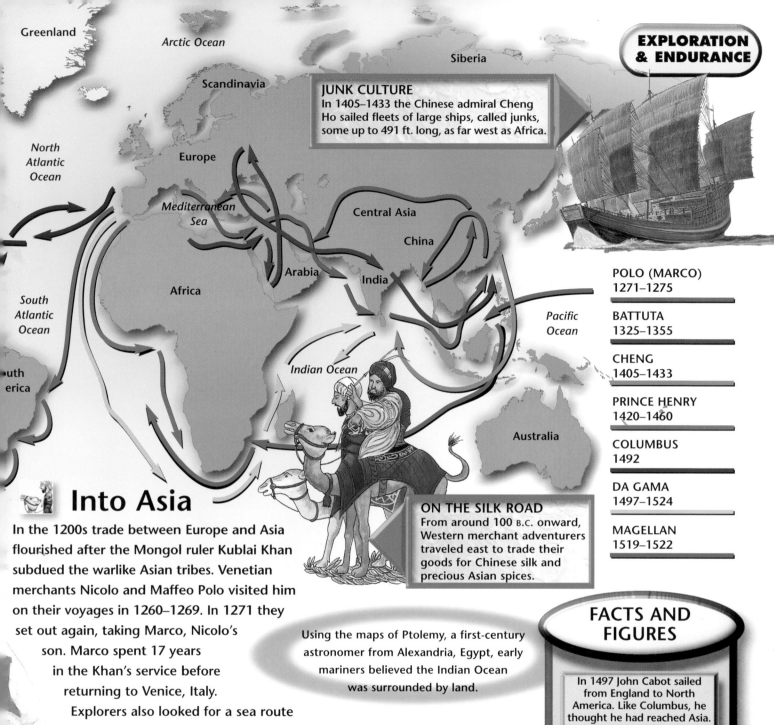

Greenland

Arctic Ocean

Siberia

Scandinavia

North Atlantic Ocean

Europe

JUNK CULTURE
In 1405–1433 the Chinese admiral Cheng Ho sailed fleets of large ships, called junks, some up to 491 ft. long, as far west as Africa.

Mediterranean Sea

Central Asia

China

Arabia

India

Africa

Pacific Ocean

South Atlantic Ocean

Indian Ocean

uth erica

Australia

POLO (MARCO) 1271–1275	
BATTUTA 1325–1355	
CHENG 1405–1433	
PRINCE HENRY 1420–1460	
COLUMBUS 1492	
DA GAMA 1497–1524	
MAGELLAN 1519–1522	

ON THE SILK ROAD
From around 100 B.C. onward, Western merchant adventurers traveled east to trade their goods for Chinese silk and precious Asian spices.

Into Asia

In the 1200s trade between Europe and Asia flourished after the Mongol ruler Kublai Khan subdued the warlike Asian tribes. Venetian merchants Nicolo and Maffeo Polo visited him on their voyages in 1260–1269. In 1271 they set out again, taking Marco, Nicolo's son. Marco spent 17 years in the Khan's service before returning to Venice, Italy.

Explorers also looked for a sea route between Europe and Asia. Vasco da Gama, a Portuguese mariner, found it. From 1497 to 1524 he took ships around the southern tip of Africa and through the Indian Ocean to India. Da Gama mistreated the Muslims and Hindus he met, but his discovery had a great impact on trade.

Using the maps of Ptolemy, a first-century astronomer from Alexandria, Egypt, early mariners believed the Indian Ocean was surrounded by land.

FACTS AND FIGURES

In 1497 John Cabot sailed from England to North America. Like Columbus, he thought he had reached Asia.

North America is named after the Spanish explorer Amerigo Vespucci, who sailed to the New World in 1497–1504.

Pytheas, a Greek navigator in the 1st century B.C., sailed to "Thule"—it was probably Iceland or Norway.

In 8th-century China some sailors spent their entire lives, from birth to death, on board huge trading ships.

HOLY TRAIL
Ibn Battuta, a young Arab from Tangier, set out in 1325 to visit Mecca. He ended up spending 30 years away! On his way to Arabia, India, Southeast Asia, China, and Africa he visited Jerusalem's Dome of the Rock (left).

GREAT ADVENTURERS

Some adventurers represent their countries, others want to set records—but most are driven by a longing for freedom or great adventures.

ON THE RIVER
French priests Jacques Marquette and Louis Jolliet traveled the Mississippi in 1673—the first Europeans to do so.

North America

By the 1500s Spain and Portugal had a stronghold on "tropical" America, but the riches they reaped soon lured in other Europeans. The British first settled in 1607 in Jamestown, Virginia. Then in 1620 the *Mayflower*, a small English sailing ship, landed in Massachusetts after a difficult 66-day voyage. Among its passengers were members of a strict religious group in search of a new way of life. They are remembered today as the Pilgrim forefathers, the founders of the Plymouth colony. The British spread out along the east coast, making treaties with the native tribes. French settlers staked claims in the vast American interior, while Spain and Russia took control of the Pacific coast. In the Revolutionary War of 1775–1783 Great Britain's colonies won their independence, and the United States was founded.

WAGONS ROLL
During the 1800s families in North America moved west to build new homes, taking all of their goods with them.

TO THE PACIFIC—AND BACK!
Sent by the U.S. president, Meriwether Lewis and William Clark left St. Louis in 1804 to explore western North America.

FACTS AND FIGURES

In 1770 Scotsman James Bruce traced the source of Africa's Blue Nile River to Lake Tana in Ethiopia.

In 1868 Germany's Gustav Nachtigal became the first European to cross the central Sahara Desert in Africa.

Europeans didn't really discover the Pacific—native people have lived on its islands for thousands of years.

Nautilus, a U.S. nuclear-powered submarine, traveled under the North Pole ice cap in August 1958.

Russian fur traders colonized Alaska in 1764 following its discovery in 1741 by Danish mariner Vitus Bering.

Pacific Ocean quests

Though the Spanish and Portuguese had been exploring the Pacific since the 1520s, it was not until 1642–1643 that Dutch Abel Tasman discovered Tasmania, New Zealand, Tonga, and the Fiji Islands. Between 1768 and 1679 English naval captain James Cook made three legendary voyages of discovery. After charting New Zealand and claiming eastern Australia for England, he sailed into the icy southern oceans. Although his third (and final) voyage to the North Pacific cost him his life, he never lost a sailor to scurvy (a vitamin C deficiency that was common to British sailors).

CLASH OF CULTURES
James Cook meets the warlike Maori of New Zealand. The sea captain was killed by natives of Hawaii in 1779.

Funded by the British Admiralty and the Royal Society, the HMS *Challenger* sailed 79,112 mi. in a survey of the Pacific in 1872–1876.

DATABANK

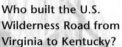

Q Which explorer brought the first French settlers to Canada?

A Jacques Cartier reached Quebec in 1534 and claimed it for France.

Q Who built the U.S. Wilderness Road from Virginia to Kentucky?

A It was built by Daniel Boone, the legendary frontiersman, in 1775.

Q Which British explorers discovered Lake Tanganyika in East Africa?

A Sir Richard Burton and John Hanning Speke explored it in 1858.

Q How did Norwegian Fridtjof Nansen make history with the *Fram*?

A His boat, the *Fram*, survived being frozen in the ice of the Arctic in the winter of 1895.

 Northern passages

For centuries European mariners sought two major goals: a trade route taking ships northeast and into Asia and a westward route "over the top" of America. There seemed to be no path through the winter ice. Finally in 1878–1880 Sweden's Nils Nordenskjold and Adolf Pander sailed through the Northeast Passage over Russia in their ship the *Vega*. Then in 1903–1906 Norwegian Roald Amundsen led a crew through the Northwest Passage around North America in his small yacht the *Gjöa*.

LOST IN THE ICE
Englishman Sir John Franklin set out for the Northwest Passage in 1845. Although he proved its existence, the intense cold and sickness killed him and his crew.

THIRD TIME LUCKY
After two failed attempts Robert Peary reached the North Pole in 1909 with African-American explorer Matt Henson.

Dutchman Willem Barents failed to sail the Northeast Passage in 1596—but the sea to the west of Alaska is named after him.

Polar heroes

Norway's Carsten Borchgrevink became one of the first people to walk on Antarctica in 1894, and in 1898–1899 he was one of the first to spend a winter there. The race was soon on to reach the South Pole. A Norwegian team, led by Roald Amundsen, arrived first in December 1911—one month ahead of a British team, led by Robert Falcon Scott. Stranded in terrible weather, the British explorers perished on their journey home.

In 1957 the British Commonwealth Trans-Antarctic Expedition, led by Vivian Fuchs, was the first to cross Antarctica.

The North Pole lies on ice, not solid land, and explorers have to travel across the frozen Arctic Ocean to reach their goal. American Frederick Cook claimed to have reached the North Pole in 1908, but he was later exposed as a liar. The glory went to fellow American Robert Peary the following year.

ICE MAN
Norway's Roald Amundsen was the greatest of all polar explorers. First to reach the South Pole and one of the first to fly over the Arctic, he died in 1928 flying to the rescue of a fellow explorer, Italian Umberto Nobile.

MUSH, MUSH!
Dog packs hauled Amundsen to the South Pole in 1911. They were more effective than the ponies used by the British team.

INTO SPACE

Space exploration first sprang from the rivalry between the United States and the Soviet Union. Today nations work together to unravel the deepest mysteries of the universe.

Space pioneers

With the Soviet launch of *Sputnik 1*, the first artificial satellite, in October 1957 the U.S.–Soviet space race had begun. In 1961 Soviet Yuri Gagarin became the first human to orbit Earth. The United States sent Alan Shepard into space a few weeks later, and in 1962 John Glenn matched Gagarin's feat. The Soviets sent the first woman, Valentina Tereshkova, into space in 1963, and Aleksei Leonov pioneered spacewalking in 1965. But by then Americans had larger goals—to send a person to the Moon.

SPUTNIK
Starting in 1957 Russia launched nine *Sputnik* satellites to test conditions in space for future manned missions.

LUNA 9
This Soviet probe made the first soft landing on the Moon in 1966—but the Soviets never put people on the Moon.

FACTS AND FIGURES

Sputnik 2, a satellite launched by the Soviet Union in 1957, successfully sent a dog named Laika into space.

The first manned international mission happened in July 1975 when a Soviet Soyuz docked with a U.S. Apollo spacecraft.

First launched in 1981, the U.S. space shuttle *Columbia* was the world's first reusable spacecraft.

All 12 men of Project Apollo who have reached the Moon have spent a collective total of 300 hours there.

To the Moon!

The Soviets made a head start in landing unmanned probes on the Moon from 1966. The American Moon program, named Project Apollo, began disastrously in 1967. The *Apollo 1* rocket burst into flames on the launchpad, killing the crew. But U.S. missions continued, many of them gathering vital information for a future landing. In 1968 American *Apollo 8* made the first manned orbit of the Moon. The following year Neil Armstrong and Buzz Aldrin made history in *Apollo 11* when they walked on the Moon.

TOUCHDOWN
Apollo 11's lunar module landed on July 20, 1969. The crew spent around two hou collecting photo and lunar rocks.

APOLLO 11 TO THE MOON
A three-stage *Saturn V* rocket carried the command and lunar modules toward the Moon at speeds of over 23,560 mph.

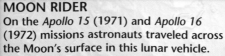

MOON RIDER
On the *Apollo 15* (1971) and *Apollo 16* (1972) missions astronauts traveled across the Moon's surface in this lunar vehicle.

Living in space

The Soviets launched their first *Salyut* space station in 1971. Tragically, after 23 days in space the crew of *Salyut 1* died when their spacecraft broke down. The United States launched their own space station, *Skylab,* in 1973 but later developed a reusable shuttle that would cut the cost of space travel. Shuttles can be used to launch satellites. Satellites are unmanned spacecraft that orbit Earth, receiving and sending information over vast distances. Satellites have many uses, from observing weather to transmitting TV signals—even spying. In 1986 the Soviet Union launched *Mir.* This space station was used by crews from all over the world until it fell back to Earth in 2001. Research now focuses on the *International Space Station* (*ISS*), a shared project between Russia, the United States, and other nations.

HOMES IN THE SKY
Future space stations are planned that will unite crews from all over the world to conduct peaceful research.

BLAST OFF!
At its launch a space shuttle carries a large tank of liquid fuel and a pair of solid fuel booster rockets. All three are released when their fuel is used up. After mission completion the shuttle glides back to Earth.

SPACE WALK
Using a space suit and jet pack, an astronaut can move in space. This is handy when working outside on new satellites launched on space shuttles.

In 2001 wealthy American Dennis Tito was the first "space tourist," paying $20 million for an eight-day visit to the *International Space Station.*

Probing the unknown

After the success of the *Sputnik* missions in the 1950s scientists planned longer probe missions. U.S. probes *Pioneer 10* and *Pioneer 11* will cruise past the two largest planets in our solar system, Jupiter and Saturn, and then continue on. *Pioneer 10* is due to reach the constellation Taurus in 300,000 years. With the chance that one day it could be found by extraterrestrials, it carries a plaque to show where it came from. *Voyager 1* and *Voyager 2* were designed primarily to explore the outer planets of the solar system. That task was completed in 1989, and they have begun to chart the heliopause, the limits of the Sun's pull. After that they will pass through interstellar space. In 2000 the *Voyager 1* probe overtook the slower *Pioneer 10*.

GALILEO AND SON
In 1995 the U.S. probe *Galileo* released a smaller probe to study the atmosphere of Jupiter, the solar system's largest planet.

DISTANT GOAL
Probes travel to planets or outer space, beyond the reach of manned spacecraft, and beam information back to scientists.

No one owns the Moon. Its independence is secure under the United Nations Treaty on Outer Space, signed in 1967.

BEYOND THE LIMITS

Everyone would love to have their name in a book of records—but for what? Stakes rise as years go by, tempting people to try even more bizarre or dangerous challenges.

FACTS AND FIGURES

Frenchman Jacques Cousteau, inventor of the Aqua-Lung in 1943, was the first to dive without a surface airpipe.

American Russ Wicks set the water speed record in 2000 in a hydroplane—a boat that almost flies—at 204 mph.

In 2001 a multinational group of cavers set a new record of reaching a depth of 5,598 ft. in the Voronya Cave in Georgia.

The wild sea

When British captain William Bligh lost his ship, the *Bounty*, to mutineers in 1789, he faced his greatest challenge ever. Without charts, he navigated the ship's longboat 4,030 mi. (6,500km) to the island of Timor. Feats of endurance continue today. England's Francis Chichester sailed solo around the world in 1966–1967, and Robin Knox-Johnston repeated that feat nonstop in 1968–1969. Then in 1994, with New Zealander Peter Blake, Knox-Johnston sailed around the world in a record 74 days, 22 hours, and 17 minutes. In 2001 England's Ellen MacArthur was the youngest woman to finish the Vendée Globe around-the-world yacht race. She was only 24.

In 2001 British Jim Shekhdar became the first person to row unassisted across the Pacific Ocean, a distance of around 8,060 mi.

Aiming high

For those of us with a fear of heights the daring feats of climbers are the most incredible of all. Englishman Edward Whymper conquered several peaks in the Alps, including the Matterhorn, between 1860–1869. The first to climb the highest mountains on all of the seven continents was Canadian Patrick Morrow, who completed this task in 1986. Six years later Australian daredevils Glenn Singleman and Nick Feteris set a record after parachuting off of the world's highest cliff face— the 20,486 ft. (6,258m) Great Trango Tower in Pakistan. Acrobats need to be fearless too. In 1859 Frenchman Charles Blondin first crossed the mighty Niagara Falls in North America on a tightrope. That year Jules Léotard invented the circus flying trapeze act.

ON BALANCE
French acrobat Charles Blondin made several tightrope walks over Niagara Falls. He often added new tricks to his act—such as eating a meal or pushing a wheelbarrow. He even tightroped blindfolded!

WORLD'S HIGHEST MOUNTAINEERS
On May 29, 1953 Edmund Hillary of New Zealand and Tenzing Norgay of Nepal reached Mount Everest's 28,965 ft. summit.

SUPERFAST SCOT
Richard Noble's jet car *Thrust II* (below) set a record of 628 mph in 1983. *Thrust SSC* went even faster in 1997.

Faster and faster

The desire to be first is matched only by the desire to be fastest. In 1944 German Rudolf Orpitz set the absolute speed record at 700 mph (1,130km/h) in a Messerschmitt Me 163 rocket plane. That was beat by U.S. pilot Charles "Chuck" Yeager in 1953. He reached 1,608 mph (2,594km/h) in a rocket-powered Bell X-1A. But this was still slow compared with the speed of 17,520 mph (28,260km/h) that Soviet cosmonaut Yuri Gagarin flew on his way to orbiting Earth in 1961. The joint holders of the world speed record are the crew of the *Apollo 10* command module. Unassisted by rocket power and drawn by gravity alone, this spacecraft tore through Earth's atmosphere at up to 24,736 mph (39,897km/h) as it returned from space in 1969.

SALT FLAT SPEEDER
In Bonneville, Utah, in 1935 England's Malcolm Cambell drove at a record speed of 298 mph.

FIRST SUPERSONIC PILOT
Chuck Yeager broke the sound barrier in 1947 in a Bell X-1. In years to come he would fly even faster.

Swiss Bertrand Piccard and English Brian Jones made the first around-the-world balloon trip in 1999 in *Breitling Orbiter III*.

DATABANK

Q The first to sail solo around the world was which Canadian mariner?

A Joshua Slocum made the voyage in 1895–1898 in *Spray*, a 95-year-old, 36 ft. fishing boat.

Q Who completed the first nonstop airplane flight across the United States?

A John MacCready and Oakley Kelly made the flight on May 2–3, 1923 in less than 27 hours.

Canadian Rick Hansen, who lost the use of his legs in a car accident in 1973, holds the wheelchair distance record—24,847 mi.

On a wing and a prayer

Since a plane first flew using its own power a century ago people have flown even farther and faster. Frenchman Louis Blériot piloted his monoplane over the English Channel in 1909—the first person to fly over the sea. American Charles Lindbergh topped that in 1927 when he made the first nonstop flight across the Atlantic from New York City to Paris, France.

Women could not be beat in aviation. England's Amy Johnson became the first woman to fly to Australia in 1930, only two years after the first man, Burt Hinkler. New Zealander Jean Batten not only beat Johnson's time by almost five days in 1934, she also made the return journey the next year. The American pilot Amelia Earhart set up the Ninety Niners, a club for female aviators, and in 1935 she was the first woman to make a solo flight from Hawaii to California.

CUSTOMIZED
The *Spirit of St. Louis*, the plane Charles Lindbergh flew across the Atlantic, had extra fuel tanks in the forward cabin so he had to look out of the side screens. The fresh air helped him stay awake on the 33.5-hour flight.

DEDICATED TO A DREAM
After crossing the Atlantic in 1932 Amelia Earhart vanished over the Pacific Ocean during her 1937 around-the-world attempt.

GLOSSARY

This section explains some of the unusual or difficult terms used in this book. The entries are arranged in alphabetical order.

GENERATOR
A generator uses mechanical power (movement) to generate electrical power. English scientist Michael Faraday built this early generator in 1831.

Architect A designer of buildings.

Astronomy The scientific study of the stars, planets, and other objects in space.

Atoms Tiny particles that make up matter. They are so small that the period at the end of this sentence contains millions of atoms. Atoms can bind with other atoms to form molecules.

Byzantium The ancient Greek city that gave its name to the Byzantine, or eastern Roman, empire.

Communism A system of political and economic organization in which people share a community's wealth according to their needs. The Soviet Union and Eastern Europe were ruled by Communist governments until the 1990s, and China, Cuba, and North Korea are still Communist-ruled.

Constitution A list of principles and laws by which a state or country is governed.

Digital An electronic way of storing data, music, and movies. CDs and DVDs contain digital data.

DNA Deoxyribonucleic acid (DNA) is the pattern of genes, unique to each living thing, that controls life functions. It is passed down from one generation to the next.

Electromagnet A magnet that is powered by an electrified wire coil. Loudspeakers, generators, and many other electrical devices contain electromagnets.

Enlightenment Popular during the 1700s, this philosophy valued reason over tradition in the human search for understanding and happiness.

Evolution The slow process during which animal and plant species change to adapt to new conditions. Scientists think all land animals, as well as humans, evolved from ancient sea creatures.

CATAMARAN
A sail- or self-powered ship with two hulls instead of the usual one. Pacific mariners built the first catamarans, a simple pair of hollowed-out logs, centuries ago.

Galaxy A giant group of stars held together by their own gravity. It is thought that there are billions of galaxies in the universe, each containing millions of stars. Our galaxy is called the Milky Way.

Genetic modification Altering the genes of a plant or animal to improve its usefulness for humans.

Genetics The study of plants and animals passing on characteristics to their offspring. Genes are molecules inside of cells that contain the inherited information.

Mesopotamia An area in Asia that was the birthplace of the world's first urban civilizations such as Sumer, Babylon, and Assyria. It is now the country of Iraq.

Middle Ages An era of history, also known as the medieval period, beginning with the fall of the western Roman empire around A.D. 500 and ending around A.D. 1450–1480 with the Renaissance.

Millennium One thousand years.

SOLAR SYSTEM
A collection of planets and their moons orbiting a star. In our own solar system the planets Mercury, Venus, Earth, Mars, Jupiter, Saturn, Uranus, Neptune, and Pluto orbit the Sun. Pluto is the farthest away.

Mosque A Muslim place of worship.

Navigator A sailor trained to plot a ship's course using sea charts, the stars, a timepiece, a compass, the weather, and ocean currents.

GEOLOGY
The scientific study of Earth—in particular the rocks. Trained geologists called volcanologists study volcanoes.

Nuclear reaction
By splitting the nuclei (centers) of many atoms a large amount of energy is released. This nuclear power is used for providing electricity and making atomic bombs.

Organism Any living thing—including all plants and animals.

Philosophy A collection of ideas or beliefs that try to make sense of the world. It is also the use or study of these ideas.

Prehistoric The history of the world before humans began writing records around 3000 B.C.

Probe An unmanned spacecraft used in astronomy to explore space.

Radio telescope An instrument, usually shaped like a large dish or an antenna, that picks up radio waves from outer space or from artificial satellites.

Recycle To transform a manufactured product back into a reusable form. Recyclable products include cardboard, glass, paper, metals, and plastics.

Reformation The 16th-century movement in Europe that led the Christians known as Protestants to break away from the pope's authority.

Religion A belief system. The major world religions are Buddhism, Christianity, Confucianism, Hinduism, Islam, Judaism, and Sikhism.

Renaissance A movement in art, literature, and science from around 1350–1550 based on a revival of ancient learning. It began in Italy.

Revolution 1: The overthrow of a government by its people. Examples are the U.S. (1775), France (1789), and Russia (1917). 2: A complete change in conditions, for example from manual to mechanical industry in England's Industrial Revolution (1760–1840).

Silicon chip A tiny electronic circuit built on a slice of silicon, used in many devices from digital watches to computers.

Species A living organism—for example, a sheep or a daisy—whose individuals can reproduce with one another.

Telecommunication Sending and receiving messages electronically—for example by phone, fax, or E-mail.

Tribunal A court of justice or another similar place of judgement.

Universe This contains everything that exists from the largest galaxy in space to the smallest particle of an atom on the head of a pin. The universe is larger than you can imagine.

Vaccine A chemical substance, usually a tiny, harmless dose of a disease, injected into the body to help build a natural defense system.

INDEX

A

abacuses 35
Aborigines, Australian 24
acupuncture 37
Age of Discovery 52
AIDS 37
aircraft 41, 59
Alexander the Great 15, 52
alphabets 6, 7
Amundsen, Roald 55
animals, first 32
animism 19
Apollo space program 56, 59
Archimedes' screw 34
architects 43
Armstrong, Louis 29
artists 24–25
Asia, exploration of 53
Asoka 15
astrolabes 34
atoms and molecules 31
Averroës 18

B

Baez, Joan 29
Baird, John Logie 6
Baker, Josephine 16
ballet 22–23
Barnardo, Thomas 17
baseball 49
basketball 49
Bauhaus 25
Bayeux Tapestry 20
Beauvoir, Simone de 18
Beethoven, Ludwig van 28–29
Bell, Alexander Graham 7
Big Bang Theory 30
Biosphere 8
Bligh, William 58
Blondin, Charles 58
blood 36–37
Bolívar, Simón 16
Bollywood 27
Bonaparte, Napoleon 15
books 6, 20, 21
Botticelli, Sandro 24
boxing 51
braille 20
bridges 44
Brown, John 16
Buddhism 15, 19, 42
buildings and monuments 42–44
Byzantine art 25

C

calendars 34
Callas, Maria 23
canals 45
capitalism 18
cars 38–39
Çatal Hüyük 9
Cecilia, St. 28
Chaplin, Charlie 26

Chou En-lai 14
Christianity 19
chronometers 34
CITES 13
cities 8, 9
civil rights movement (U.S.) 12–13
Clausewitz, Karl von 15
clocks and watches 34
clones 33
coins 10
Colosseum 42
Columbus, Christopher 52, 54
commerce 10–11
communication 6–7
communism 18
companies, giant 11
composers 28
computers 7, 35
Constantine 15
continents 32
Cook, James 54
Copernicus, Nicolaus 32
Cousteau, Jacques 58
cowboys 9
crafts 25
credit cards 10
Curie, Marie 31
cycling 51

D

dams 44–45
dance 23
Darling, Grace 16
Darwin, Charles 33
DDT 9
death penalty 12
democracy 18
Diderot, Denis 18
dinosaurs 26, 32
directors, movie 27
disease 37
Disney, Walt 27
DNA 33
Dylan, Bob 29

E

Earth 32–33
E-commerce 10
Edison, Thomas 35
Egyptians, ancient 36, 38, 42
Einstein, Albert 30–31
electrons 31
Elgar, Edward 28
Elizabeth I 14
Ellington, "Duke" 29
empires 14
euro (currency) 11
evolution 33
exploration 52–57

F

Faraday, Michael 30, 35
farming 8–9
fission, nuclear 31
flight 41, 59
food and shelter 8–9

football 48–49
Formula One 50–51
Francis of Assisi, St. 17
Frank, Anne 16
Franklin, Benjamin 30
French Revolution 13
Freud, Sigmund 18
fusion, nuclear 31

G

Gagarin, Yuri 56, 59
Gaia hypothesis 33
Galen of Pergamum 36
Galileo 30, 32
Garibaldi, Giuseppe 16
Gaulle, Charles de 14
genetics 33
Geneva Convention 12
geology 33
Ghandi, Mohandas K. 14
Gilbert, William 30
Gogh, Vincent van 25
golf 51
Gorbachev, Mikhail 14
Great Eastern (ship) 40
Great Wall of China 45
Greeks, ancient 18, 19, 22, 25, 36, 42, 46, 53
guillotine 13
Gutenberg, Johannas 20

H

Hammurabi 12
Hannibal 15
Hanno of Carthage 52
Hanseatic League 11
Harappa 9
helicopters 41
heroes 16–17
Hinduism 19, 42
Hippocrates 36
Hitchcock, Alfred 27
hockey 47–49
horse racing and riding 50
human rights 13

I

Ibn Battuta 53
Impressionism 24–25
Incas 6, 38
Independence, U.S. Declaration of 12
industry 34
instruments, musical 19, 28
integrated circuits 35
Internet 6, 7, 10
inventions 34–35
Islam 12, 19, 42

J

Jackson, Thomas "Stonewall" 15
jazz 29
Jenner, Edward 37
Joan of Arc 16
Judaism 19

K

Kabuki theater	23
Khan, Genghis	14, 45
Khan, Kublai	53
King, Jr., Martin Luther	13
Klee, Paul	25
Koran	12

L

language	6
Lao Tzu	15
Lawrence, T. E.	16
laws and justice	12–13
laws, universal	30–31
LCD watches	34
leaders	14–15
life, first	32–33
light	30
lightbulbs	35
Lincoln, Abraham	14
Linnaeus, Carl	33
literature	20–21
Live Aid	17
Louis XIV, King	22
Luther, Martin	19

M

McDonald's restaurants	11
machines	34
Machu Picchu	9
maglev trains	39
Magna Carta	12
man, early	8, 9, 20
Mandela, Nelson	14
Marconi, Guglielmo	7
Marshall Plan	10
Marx, Karl	18
medicine	36–37
Mendel, Gregor	33
Michelangelo	25
microscopes	36
milk	9
mime	23
Mississippi River	54
Mona Lisa (painting)	24
money	10–11
Moon	56–57
Morse Code	7
Moses	15
motors, electric	35
mountaineers	58
movies	26–27
Mozart, Wolfgang Amadeus	28
Mughals	14
music	28–29
myths	19

N

Navratilova, Martina	51
Newton, Isaac	30
Nicklaus, Jack	51
Nightingale, Florence	17
Norse gods	19
North America, colonies	54
Northeast and Northwest passages	55

novels	21
nuclear power	31
Nuremberg Trials	12

O

oil reserves	11
Olivier, Laurence	22
Olympic Games	46–47
opera	23

P

Pacific Ocean, explored	54
painters	24–25
Panama Canal	45
Pankhurst, Emmeline	13
Pasteur, Louis	37
patents	10, 35
PCs	35
pens, ballpoint	35
philosophies and religions	18–19
Phoenicians	11, 52
Picasso, Pablo	24
planets	57
plants, genetically modified	8
plate tectonics	32
Plato	18
plows	8
poetry	20
polar expeditions	54–55
Polo, Marco	53
popes	15
printing presses	20
Ptolemy	32, 53
pyramids	42

R

radiation, electromagnetic	30
radio	7
rail	38–39
rainbows	30
record breakers	58–59
Red Cross	17
Reformation	19
religion	15, 19, 42
Renaissance	24–25
roads	38
rockets	56
Romans, ancient	10, 12, 14, 22, 38, 42

S

Saladin	15
Sargon of Akkad	14
satellites, artificial	7, 56
Schumacher, Michael	51
science, laws of	30–31
sculptors	25
scurvy	37
Shakespeare, William	22
ships and boats	40, 58
Silk Road	53
sitars	28
Sitting Bull	16
skeletons	36
skyscrapers	44
slavery	13, 16

soccer	48–49
sound barrier	59
Soviet Union	18
space exploration	56–57
space probes	57
space shuttles	56–57
space stations	57
speed records	59
Spirit of St. Louis (aircraft)	59
sports	46–51
statespeople	14
Statue of Liberty	43
Stephenson, George	39
stethoscopes	37
Stonehenge	34, 35, 42
submarines	40, 54
submersibles	58
Suez Canal	45
surgery	37
Suu Kyi, Aung San	16
Sydney Opera House	43

T

Taj Mahal	43
Taoism	15
telecommunications	7
telephones	7, 35
telescopes, radio	45
television	6, 7
tennis	50–51
Teresa, Mother	17
theater	22–23
Tibet	42
time	34
Tocqueville, Alexis de	18
track and field	50
trade	10–11
transplants, heart	37
transportation	38–41
tunnels	45

U/V

United Nations	12
vaccination	37
Venice	9
Vesalius, André	36
Vietnam War	17
Vikings	52
Vinci, Leonardo da	24, 35, 41
voting	13, 18

W/X

Wailing Wall	43
Walesa, Lech	17
Wallace, William	16
walls	45
Watt, James	34
Wegener, Alfred	32
wheels	34
World War II	17
Wren, Christopher	43
Wright, Orville and Wilbur	41
writing	6–7
X rays	36

ACKNOWLEDGMENTS

The publishers would like to thank the following:

Artists & contributors

Every effort has been made to trace and credit the artists whose work appears in this book, and the publishers apologize to those whose names do not appear below:

Simone Boni, Vincent Wakerley, Nicki Palin, Marion Appleton, Chris Forsey, Andie Peck, R. Berridge, Terry Gabbey, Linden Artists Ltd., Christian Hook, Chris Molan, Ron Tiner, Chris Turnbull, Melvyn Pickering, Peter Dennis, Clive Spong, Richard Hook, Chris Lyon, Kate Maddison, Venessa Card, Tom Connell, Mike Roffe, Richard Ward, Peter Bull, Mark Bergin, John James, Sebastian Quigley, Adam Hook, Ian Jackson, Eric Rowe, Nick Harris, Biz Hull, Martin Reiner, Dave Etchell, John Rudyard, Aswain Bell, Martin Knowlden, Rodney Shackell, J. Gower, David Sabriya, Shirley Willis, Guy Smith, Roger Hutchings, Luigi Galante, John Scorey Susanna Addario, Andre Hrydziusko, D. Fletcher, Mike Lacey, Tony Smith, Bernard Robinson, Peter Jones, Kevin Maddison, David Russel

Contributors: Robert Cave, Fergus Collins, Catrin Edwards, Ben Hoare, Chris Moss, Kay Ollerenshaw, Kate Turner, John Woodward

Photographs

b=bottom, c=center, l=left, t=top

p. 21(bl) Bettmann/CORBIS; p. 22(bl) Bettmann/CORBIS; p. 23(tl) James Marshall/CORBIS; p. 24(cr & cl) Historical Picture Archive/CORBIS, Francis G. Mayer/CORBIS; p. 25(tl) Burnstein Collection/CORBIS; p. 26(cl & bl) Bettmann/CORBIS, Mitchell Gerber/CORBIS; p. 27(c) Bettmann/CORBIS; p. 29(cl) Henry Diltz/CORBIS; p. 43(c) Yann Arthus-Bertrand/CORBIS(c); p. 47(cl & cr & bl) Richard Hamilton Smith/CORBIS, Duomo/CORBIS, Joel W. Rogers/CORBIS; p. 48(cl & br) TempSport/CORBIS, Wally McNamee/CORBIS; p. 49(cr) Scott Wachter/CORBIS; p. 50(c) Bettmann/CORBIS; p. 51(cl & cr) S. Carmona/ CORBIS, Tony Roberts/CORBIS; p. 55(cr) Bettmann/ CORBIS; p. 58(cr) Hulton-Deutsch Collection/CORBIS

The following images are courtesy of *The Illustrated London News*: p. 7(tr); p. 12(br); p. 13(tr); p. 14(tl); p. 16(bl); p. 17(cl); p. 18(cl & bl); p. 21(br); p. 24(br); p. 26(bc & tr); p. 28(cr); p. 30(bl); p. 31(bl); p. 37(tr); p. 38(cl); p. 40(cr); p. 41(tr); p. 45(br); p. 46(cl); p. 47(tr); p. 48(bl); p. 50(bl); p. 55(cl & br); p. 59(bl & tr)

THE FUTURE
Earth's population is expected to peak in 2050 at around 12 billion. In order to keep all of us fed until then, the planet has to yield as much food as it has ever done throughout human history— quite a feat!